Sustainable Service

Sustainable Service

Adi Wolfson

 BUSINESS EXPERT PRESS

First published in 2016 by
Business Expert Press, LLC
222 East 46th Street, New York, NY 10017
www.businessexpertpress.com

ISBN-13: 978-1-63157-461-0 (paperback)
ISBN-13: 978-1-63157-462-7 (e-book)

Business Expert Press Service Systems and Innovations in Business and Society Collection

Collection ISSN: 2326-2664 (print)
Collection ISSN: 2326-2699 (electronic)

Cover and interior design by S4Carlisle Publishing Services Private Ltd., Chennai, India

First edition: 2016

10 9 8 7 6 5 4 3 2 1

Printed in the United States of America

Abstract

Service and the service dominant logic driving today's global economy influence every aspect of our lives, in the process, shaping our social and natural environments. This scenario dictates that new ways to provide services must be offered that will enrich service systems and service networks with added values and benefits, ultimately to yield sustainable services.

To put sustainability into practice and generate sustainable services will require more than merely implementing efficient physical resource management in the production, delivery, and use of services. First and foremost, sustainable service is that which fulfills customer needs and can be perpetuated for long periods of time without negatively influencing the customer's natural or social environment. In addition, sustainable services should integrate smart use of nonphysical resources with environmentally and socially aware behaviour, and take into account the service's potential short- and long-term effects, on both the local and the global scales.

As service systems and networks will undoubtedly become much more complex and specific in the future, they will require better coordination of the various actors, whether human or not, and better synchronization of the value production and delivery processes. These services should comprise three levels: (1) unidirectional value exchange from supplier to consumer, (2) bidirectional value co-creation between provider and customer, and (3) return of values by simultaneous co-generation of direct and indirect values by a provider and a customer to other customers (i.e., 3D services). Finally, the production of 3D services will enable the provision of long-term and indirect values and the co-creation of values with many indirect actors and even with the next generations. Moreover, sustainable services will be based on the generation of environmental, social, and economic values integrated into the provision of sustainability as a value, resembling the provision of ecosystem services.

Keywords

Carbon footprint, CleanServ, Smart city, Service, Sustainability

Contents

Preface

Service and the service dominant logic driving today's global economy influence every aspect of our lives, in the process, shaping our social and natural environments. This scenario dictates that new ways to provide services must be offered that will enrich service systems and service networks with added values and benefits, ultimately to yield sustainable services.

A sustainable service necessarily comprises environmental, social, and economic values, which are designed, produced, and delivered in concert. It should also identify and analyze the external forces that affect the macro environment of each service (e.g., using STEEP analysis that accounts for the social, technological, economic, environmental, and political dimensions of those forces). In general terms, the sustainability of a service is built on the rational use of physical and nonphysical resources across both time and space, and as such, it must account not only for long- and short-term effects, but also for those at the local and global scales. Thus, to achieve the ultimate goal of sustainable service, each service's core- and super-values—from the transfer of values from supplier to consumer, to the co-creation of values between provider and customer, to the co-generation of values by the provider and the customer for other stakeholders—must be imbued with sustainability.

This book first outlines the parallel development of service science and sustainability science from their early days to the present while summarizing the main paradigms, concepts, and terminologies in both fields. The second part of the book discusses the reciprocal relationship between sustainability and service in depth while offering a variety of ways by which environmental, social, and economic values can be introduced into service provision to provide sustainability as service. Finally, it also presents examples of how sustainability can be introduced in the shareconomy and smart city frameworks, and it looks ahead to the next generation of services and considers how sustainability and service will interact in the future.

Adi Wolfson

Acknowledgments

I would first like to thank the series editors, Jim Spohrer and Haluk Demirkan, for offering me the opportunity to write this book. I would also like to thank Patrick Martin for editing the text and assisting me in clarifying my thoughts. At last, I want to acknowledge the generous support of Sami Shamoon College of Engineering, which enabled me to perform the in-depth research in the field of sustainable service that was necessary to complete the book.

CHAPTER 1

The "Evolution" of Service and Sustainability

The Beginning

The creation of the world, whether by the "big bang" or by force majeure, defined the dimensions of space and time and produced the physical resources that together constitute our planet. This was followed by a series of extended and complex evolutionary processes characterized by changes in energy and material that shaped the natural environment into the form we recognize today and which define the animate and inanimate worlds. With the emergence of the human race, revolutionary processes driven by changes in technology and in how human beings comprehend themselves and their surroundings led to social, economic, and environmental changes with far-reaching consequences.

To sustain life, nature produces and supplies in concert a variety of products that can be roughly categorized as physical resources or tangible values (i.e., goods such as air, water, food, and minerals) or nonphysical resources or intangible values (i.e., services like pollination and temperature regulation). From the dawn of humanity, humankind survived by exploiting these resources, which were provided via myriad natural processes that today are collectively known as *ecosystem services* (Figure 1.1) (Gretchen 1997). These can be divided into the four general categories of provisioning, regulating, supporting, and cultural services (Table 1.1). Most natural processes are cyclic, which ensures that minimal amounts of materials and energy are used and/or lost and that resources are regenerated.

Although each ecosystem service category refers to specific natural processes, they are intricately intertwined in terms of both function and output. Provisioning services are all the tangible goods produced by

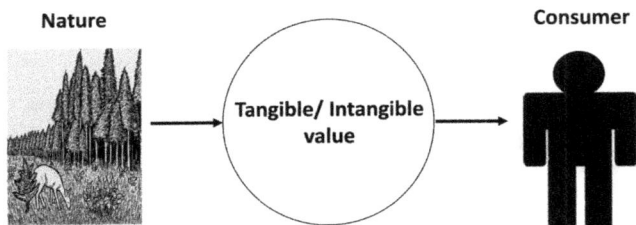

Figure 1.1 Ecosystem services

Table 1.1 Ecosystem service categories

Category	Examples
Provisioning	Water, food, fibers, wood, fuel, biochemicals
Regulating	Temperature regulation, water regulation, erosion control, flood control, disease control, detoxification
Supporting	Nutrient cycle, pollination, soil formation, primary production, habitat, waste decomposition, water and air purification
Cultural	Aesthetics, recreation, spiritual, communal, educational

ecosystems—from raw materials and food to pharmaceuticals and genes. In parallel, nature also provides intangible regulating services such as climate regulation, waste decomposition, and disease control. These material and nonmaterial values are backed by supporting services, like nutrient recycling, pollination, and water and air purification, all of which are essential to perpetuate the production and delivery of all other services. Finally, in contrast to the first three categories—which reference naturally occurring processes that happen regardless of whether there is a human presence—the category of cultural services relies on people's perception. Thus, nature also supplies cultural services in the forms of spiritual and esthetic experiences that enrich and develop people's cognitive selves as well as their social and cultural lives.

From the beginnings of the human race, with the appearance of the first human species (i.e., Homo genus) about 2.5 million years ago, ecosystem services also determined people's way of life. The earliest human societies comprised hunter-gatherers whose survival depended on their daily collection of goods—from water and food to stone tools and shelters—directly from nature. Moreover, people also had to exploit nature's intangible provisions, and in the process, they molded their life course according to the natural order reflected in the cyclicality of day and night and the seasons of the year. As such, the members of the wanderer-forager society were actually ecosystem service consumers, and all natural goods and services were delivered in a one-sided, unidirectional mode (Figure 1.1). Nonetheless, though people did not produce their own goods, they had to create their own intangible values, which later were termed services, to fulfill their own needs or those of their family or group members. These early services, which entailed the utilization of the natural resources in their environments, included such activities as food gathering, residence guarding, and raising children. Although all the members of early human societies could have performed these human-made services, the corresponding tasks were usually assigned to different group members based on gender and age. Finally, in their consumption of ecosystem services, people also supplied nature with various services in return, such as the thinning of flora and the transportation of seeds from place to place.

The hunter-gatherer way of life also determined what would later come to be known as the primary sector of the economy (i.e., the collection of raw materials from nature and their processing into products). This virgin economic activity, the extraction and harvesting of nature's goods from the earth coupled with related services, was based on the *value* of each good or service. That value, which was associated with the importance of the goods and services to the maintenance of life, was bounded by natural resources and human labor, and entailed minimal use of technology. Moreover, the economic model during that period of human history was based on the collection and use of resources in an efficient process that necessarily let little go to waste. Thus, the hunter-gatherer lifestyle also forged an intuitive connection between people and nature that fostered a harmonic and symbiotic mutual relationship between the two.

Human Revolution

Characterized by the emergence of language, the first big revolution, termed the *human revolution* or the *language revolution*, happened around 70,000 years ago, and it also led to the development of consciousness and conscience (Mellars and Stringer, 1989). Though people had already been communicating through voice and gestures for thousands of years, the dawn of language significantly altered the intensity and quality of communication between people, and as a result, they began to gather in larger groups, although they continued to live as wanderers in an economic system based on the hunter-gatherer lifestyle. In addition, these new communication abilities acquired by the human race led first to the worldwide migration of the wise person (i.e., Homo sapiens), who had begun to evolve around 130,000 years ago, and then, around 40,000 years ago, to the appearance of the most developed human subspecies, modern humans (Homo sapiens sapiens).

The language revolution changed the social fabric of human life insofar as it allowed humans to share social information, a skill upon which neither their physical lives nor their basic evolutionary drives to survive and reproduce depended. Moreover, group living, which required certain codes of conduct, also raised moral issues that grew out of the need to take the interests of one's fellow group members into consideration. Though morality is probably as old as humanity, the human revolution added social values to the nascent economic values (i.e., goods and services). Loosely defined as the criteria people use to assess their daily lives, to arrange their priorities, and to choose between alternative courses of action (Friedman and Kahn Jr. 2002), social values provided general guidelines for social conduct, formed an important part of the culture of the society, and accounted for the stability of social order. In addition to its social ramifications, the human revolution also changed the quality and intensity of human-made services, which are in fact based on personal contact, and in the process, people delivered novel services that were not directly associated with the maintenance of physical life. Finally, from an environmental point of view, the human revolution modified the notion of human superiority, and despite their revised perception of their surroundings, people began to feel alienated from nature. Later, the human revolution not only altered the balance between the relative quantities of ecosystem services that humans consumed and services exchanged between people, it also marked the point at which people began to investigate and criticize nature.

Agricultural Revolution

The dynamic relationship between humans and their natural world was inexorably altered by the *Neolithic Revolution* or the first *Agricultural Revolution* around 12,000 years ago (Barker 2009). Characterized by the domestication of plants and animals, the agricultural revolution added to the role humans played, from that solely of food consumers to also include the production of food. It changed people's lifestyle from that of nomadic hunter-gatherers to the more sedentary lives of farmers living in permanent settlements who were able to produce everything for their own needs as well as for those of others. The agricultural revolution also signaled an advance in human-generated services, introducing new services such as storage, sale, trade, and administration, which were usually coupled with the production of goods. This monumental shift in human society also led to a distinction, for the first time, between the production of tangible and intangible values. Thus it effected social and economic changes by expanding the primary sector of the economy from natural-based products to those produced by humans. The relative abundance and variety of food that accompanied the agricultural revolution expanded the meaning of *economic-value* from the extent to which a good was needed to sustain life to include the utility of the good or its *use-value* (Gibbins 1976). These changes also led to a crucial transition from an economy that was based mainly on ecosystem provisions to a barter-based paradigm defined by the direct exchange of goods or services for other goods or services and in which everyone is simultaneously a supplier and a consumer. Thus, each value also had an *exchange-value* representing its trade or market value.

From a social perspective, the prosperity and luxuries afforded by the agricultural revolution together with the greater amounts of free time enjoyed by people encouraged the development of new professions. Yet this new lifestyle also entailed undesirable tradeoffs, for example, it redefined the concept of labor or division of labor. Thus, on an average, agriculturalists performed more work than nomads, on the one hand, but on the other, farming required less cooperation and sharing than hunting and gathering. Some families were therefore able to provide for themselves by farming their own lands or by using laborers or slaves to do that work, and this eventually led to the creation of social classes that, in turn, engendered societal conflict. In addition, despite the abundance and seeming prosperity facilitated by the agricultural revolution, its focus on a sedentary lifestyle supported with domestic crops and animals changed the components of people's nutrition almost overnight—resulting in a decline in overall levels of health—and also led to drastic changes in the quality and level of daily activity. Moreover, life in permanent settlements exposed people to diseases associated with living amidst one's own waste and with domestic animals and to a marked increase in the risks of drought, flood, and fire. Finally, although agriculturlism indeed led to prosperity, insofar as it necessitated abandoning a nomadic existence in favor of staying put in settlements, it also created insecurity and increased one's susceptibility to attack. People responded to the increased threat to their security by accelerating the building of settlements and by creating essential new services such as guarding.

The agricultural revolution also had a significant impact on the natural environment, and paradoxically, the more people turned to farming and experienced a new kind of connection with their natural environment, the farther, in fact, they became from nature. In mimicking nature, people manipulated and exploited it in myriad ways. Indeed, the agricultural revolution marked the first time that humans ruled, or attempted to rule, nature, in the process effectively separating themselves from their natural environment as if they were in control. Inevitably, farming altered the landscape of the world as land was rapidly expropriated from nature while for the first time, distinctions were made between natural and violated areas and between public and private areas. Vast quantities of natural resources were consumed in the process, which also increased soil exhaustion and ultimately disrupted natural selection. The large amounts of water and nutrients required to perpetuate an agriculturally-based society led people to divert natural resources such as rivers. Such engineering feats ultimately had detrimental effects on the environment, which manifested in changes to the natural cycles and balance of local ecosystems that harmed biodiversity along the river's path and even resulted in some rivers running dry. Finally, the permanent settlements facilitated by the agricultural revolution also caused previously unheard of environmental damage. From the vast quantities of wastewater and waste produced by settlements of people to the massive use of trees to build and heat their dwellings, these phenomena gradually led to the development of new perspectives and philosophies regarding the mutual relationship between nature and humanity. In the latter part of the agricultural revolution, that newfound understanding expressed by some sparked primarily local attempts at environmental protection—from efforts to balance lumber use with the planting of new trees to the formation of nature reserves and animal protection societies—to save and protect what they now understood was their natural heritage (Wiersum 1995).

Although prior to the agricultural revolution all human-made services were produced in conjunction with ecosystem services, later, many services were produced and delivered indirectly (e.g., seeds sowed by people instead of naturally spread or human made water reservoirs). Furthermore, though many services like marketing and storing were still performed in a series, after the goods were produced, many new, standalone services, like administrative and management services, were created for the first time. Finally, in the late stages of the agricultural revolution, the barter economy became more developed, and a *value in-exchange* economic mode was defined (Humphrey and Hugh-Jones 1992). According to this model, value is produced and delivered by a supplier to a client in exchange for another value, and later on, in exchange for money (Figure 1.2). The roots of a system of commodity money, whose value was based on the commodity from which it was made, for example gold, silver, or tea, date to around 3000 BC in Mesopotamia, while representative money and the use of coins began around 600 BC.

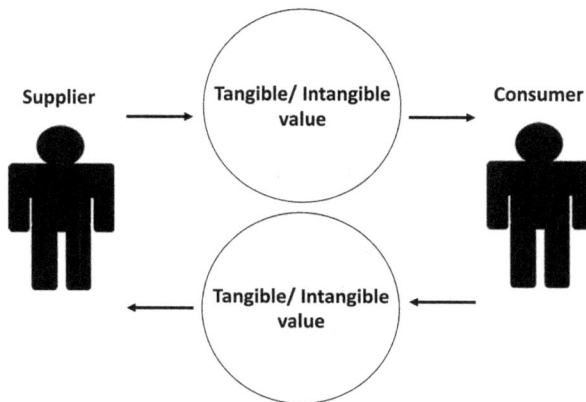

Figure 1.2 Value in-exchange model

The agricultural revolution also marked a period in human history during which the collective knowledge of human society grew tremendously. The subsequent need for management and administrative services to facilitate trade and for the establishment of central authorities constituted what was probably the main driving force behind the emergence of writing, about 4000 years ago, which, in turn, ushered humans from prehistory into the age of written and documented history. Additionally, the final stages of the first agricultural revolution witnessed the birth of monotheistic religions as well as western Greek philosophy and eastern philosophies like Buddhism and Taoism. Both religion, a social-cultural organization under a collection of beliefs, views, norms, and collective rules, and philosophy, the study of fundamental truths and principles of being, knowledge, and conduct, tremendously altered how human beings perceived themselves and their social and natural environments. Moreover, they also prompted people to inquire about the origins of the world and humanity, and to the economic and social values of goods and services, they added the notion of *ethical-value*, which comprises morals. From the ethical-value perspective, the concept of value also prioritizes goods, services, and actions or behavior according to their importance to individuals or to society, and it is used as a tool that aids decision making about right and wrong or good and bad, ultimately playing a large part in determining our behavior. Finally, the expansion of knowledge and the emergence of religion and philosophy spurred the rise of a variety of new services, such as education, medicine, and entertainment. Previously, these services had been practiced and transferred to some extent within the family mainly to prepare the young with the knowledge and skills necessary to survive, but by the end of the agricultural revolution, they had become integral parts of society.

Finally, both religion and philosophy address the mutual relationship between people and their surroundings and the effects of human actions and lifestyle on nature. Representative examples can be found in the biblical stories of the Garden of Eden and Noah's Ark, the concept of yin and yang in Chinese philosophy, and the questions asked about the essence of the physical world and human beings in the works of Plato (e.g., *Timaeus Dialogue*) and Aristotle (e.g., *On the Soul* [de Anima]).

Scientific and Industrial Revolutions

The next big revolution, the *Scientific Revolution*, which emerged in the 16th century during the early modern period, in fact continues to shape human society to this day (Shapin 1996). Initially characterized by a fundamental transformation in the prevailing scientific ideas and methods, it radically altered the natural sciences (e.g., physics, mathematics, and chemistry). Insofar as it distinguished between the physical world and metaphysics with respect to ideas about things that are seemingly beyond the corporeal world, the scientific revolution changed how people perceived their social and natural environments. It also generated the invention of innovative and groundbreaking technologies, central among them the steam engine, which marked the beginning of *Industrial Revolution* at the end of the 18th century (Lucas 2002).

With the industrial revolution, for the first time knowledge was transferred from theory to action and was accessible to the public. Forever changing people's lifestyles, the industrial revolution also led to rigorous developments in the economic, social, and environmental processes that began during the agricultural revolution. Besides the mass production of food via mechanized processes that led to an excess of goods and expanded trade activities, the industrial revolution also promoted the production of synthetic materials such as fibers. In addition, it marked the dawn of a new era characterized by the production of merchandise in great variety that was not necessary for the physical needs of human survival and that, in contrast to food, was produced indirectly from nature.

The industrialized mass production of goods brought about by the industrial revolution shifted the focus of the economy from that based on tedious hand labor and established the second sector of the economy (i.e., industry), which used primary sector output as its raw materials. Correspondingly, the labor market and marketing and trade also evolved, and the increased production of low use-value goods that were not necessary for existence but that had high exchange-value stressed the fundamental differences between the two value systems and the monumental changes that people were experiencing in their lifestyles.

The social inequality and instability that characterized the end of the Neolithic period were exacerbated during the industrial revolution; that combined with new radical and liberal political ideas being voiced at the time with the development of socio-economic systems such as socialism initiate the decline of monarchal systems and their eventual replacement with republics (e.g., the French Revolution). Changes in the labor market led to increased incomes for many workers, a scenario that promoted greater overall social satisfaction. This increase in prosperity, in turn, helped fuel population growth and urbanization, which is characterized by a built environment outfitted with the necessary infrastructures and social systems, and it also initiated the consumption culture that today continues to define the role of people as consumers.

Although the industrial revolution cemented people's reliance on natural and synthetic goods, and constituted goods as the dominant logic of marketing (i.e., *good dominant logic*), it also promoted an expansion of the service sector that continued in the 19th and 20th centuries. Moreover, increased urbanization and the development of systems of governance during this period dictated the creation of many new public and civil services. However, most of the services were generic and mimicked the value in-exchange model of the production and delivery of goods.

The massive changes of the industrial revolution that redefined social and economic systems and that altered people's lifestyles also caused serious environmental degradation. With industrialization came the expeditious and often abusive use of natural resources and the increased production of effluents and wastes. Thus, their exploitation and manipulation of the natural environment further distanced people from nature, and some began to notice undesirable environmental changes manifested by the sudden scarcity or total loss of some parts of the natural resource base. People's realization that natural resources are limited eventually formed the basis of environmentalism (i.e., environmental philosophy, ideology, and activity), the seeds for which were sown during the *Romantic Period* at the end of the 18th century.

A movement driven by intellectuals and artists, romanticism emphasized the uniqueness of nature and of every person together with the importance of maintaining one's appreciation of and connection with nature. Thus, it called for a return to nature and a renewal of the mutual relationship between nature and humanity. The emphasis of romanticism on the natural environment led to the creation of a new type of value, termed *environmental-value.* Taking the perspective that nature has a right to thrive, environmental-value stressed the necessity to distinguish between right and wrong resource utilization, on the one hand, and to invest effort in quantifying environmental damage to learn how it can be regulated and controlled, on the other hand.

The exponential growth in human knowledge that began with the industrial revolution fostered the emergence of new technologies that in turn spawned additional revolutions. The *Second Industrial Revolution* or the *Technological Revolution* was another great leap forward in technology that promoted the expansion of electricity, petroleum, and steel and that had a marked influence on society as a whole (Hall 1995). This was followed by the *Third Industrial Revolution* or the *Digital Revolution,* which was characterized by advances in technology as analog electronic and mechanical devices were replaced with digital technology (Rifkin 2008). Finally, the *Information and Communication Revolution/Age,* in which we all live, refers to the expansion of information transfer and to the broad range of computer and communications equipment that enabled it (Foster and Wood 1997; Santangelo 2001). Each of these revolutions and their corresponding technological leaps have effected significant changes not only in people's lifestyles and on societies, but also on the global economy and the environment. They also completely changed not only the way that we produce, deliver, and use services, but also the role and the share of the service sector in the economy (i.e., the tertiary sector of economy), and in so doing, they redefined the essence of services.

Service Revolution

Though services have been produced by nature and people since antiquity, service was classified as the tertiary sector of economy, and until recently, it was defined mainly in terms of everything that is *not* agriculture or manufacturing (i.e., the "soft" part of economy) as it supplies intangible values. This relegation of service to a less significant role than the other sectors of the economy was due in part to it traditionally being the smallest sector of the economy, in which typically services were not stand-alone and were mostly provided in conjunction with goods. Moreover, in contrast to the primary and secondary sectors of the economy, the service sector was not perceived as critical to human survival. Finally, until recently, services were less easy to trade and less competitive than goods, and therefore, they entailed higher costs. Over the last 100 years, however, the economy has undergone massive change manifested in the shift from a heavy reliance on agriculture and manufacturing to a greater emphasis on services. Evidence of this transformation is expressed in the increased share of the service sector in the workforce and in the gross domestic products (GDPs) of countries. Today, services constitute the largest and the fastest growing sector of the western economy, which is also sometimes referred to as a *service economy*.

The emerging significance of the service sector and the corresponding ascension of service as the dominant logic in marketing and as the fundamental basis of exchange led Vargo and Lush in 2004 to define *service dominant logic* (Vargo and Lush 2004, 2008; Lush and Vargo 2006). Describing economies as fundamentally based on services and goods that function as distribution mechanisms for service provision, this paradigm replaces the good dominant logic that focused on industrial-based products or manufactured outputs. Instead, analogous to the conceptualization of ecosystem services, service dominant logic emphasizes the importance to the economy of the intangible values provided by services. Vargo and Lush also suggested ten foundational premises to define the framework of service dominant logic.

In parallel with the emergence of service dominant logic, IBM initiated research into service and social engineering systems, beginning the field of *service science*. Moreover, to better define the goal of service science and to promote service innovation, IBM launched a multidisciplinary academic endeavor it termed *service science, management, and engineering (SSME)* (IBM Almaden Services Research 2006). Several years later, when service became more complex and comprehensive and necessarily involved numerous disciplines and stakeholders, service science became a platform for the systematic study, development and implementation of services and innovation (Spohrer et al., 2007; Maglio and Spohrer 2007; Maglio, Kieliszewski, and Spohrer 2010).

The shift toward a service economy, known as tertiarization, and the conceptualization of the new frameworks of service dominant logic and service science, defined service according to what it is and what it is not (i.e., everything that is not agriculture or manufacture [Wolfson et al., 2010]) and planted the seeds for the *Service Revolution*. To further characterize services and highlight the differences between services and goods, service science lists four general characteristics to define a service:

1. *intangibility*: service can neither be seen nor touched, and it is based mainly on nonphysical resources.
2. *inseparability*: service is simultaneously produced, delivered and consumed, thereby requiring direct interaction between the supplier and the consumer.
3. *perishability*: service can neither be stored nor returned as tangible value, and all the resources associated with the service are available for a definite time during service delivery.
4. *heterogeneity*: service cannot be repeated in exactly the same way each time it is performed, as it depends not only on the supplier and the client, but also on the place and the time of provision.

Finally, the service revolution also redefined and altered the value production and delivery process, replacing the value in-exchange model with the *value in-use* model and exchanging the roles of supplier and consumer with those of provider and customer (Figure 1.3). The value in-use model is based on a value *co-creation* process, according to which a provider and a customer use and share a constellation of integrated resources and capabilities to produce and deliver the value. Under the value in-use paradigm, therefore, the supplier is replaced with a provider that, in addition

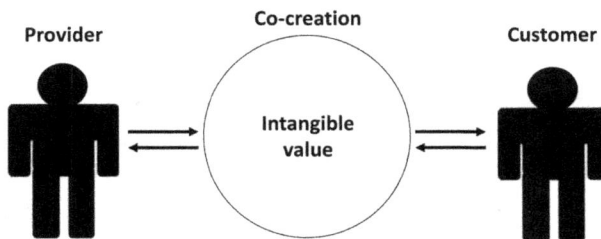

Figure 1.3 Value in-use model

to transferring supplies, provides a platform for the production and de-livery of the value to the customer. Likewise, in contrast to the consumer, who plays a passive role in the value in-exchange model, the customer has an active role in the value provision process. Finally, the main incentive behind the service revolution was not only to foster the emergence of new technologies, but also to promote significant social and environmental change. In turn, the service revolution also had myriad effects on both the social and natural environments.

With the maturation of the service dominant logic approach and the desire to add human factors to service engineering (Freund and Cel-lary 2014), values became well defined, tailored to each customer, and human-centric. However, the generation and delivery of value needed to be more efficient, productive, and satisfying. Moreover, because value co-creation usually involves multiple actors (Prahalad and Ramaswamy 2004), among whom are unique, reciprocal links, the *value in-context* model was proposed (Figure 1.4) (Chandler and Vargo 2011). Based on the idea that *where* value creation happens is important, the value in-context approach dictates that the relevant actors involved in the delivery and consumption of a service be synchronized in the creation and delivery of that service from the provider to the customer. It thus not only expanded the definition of provider and added co-providers to the process, it also assigned more responsibility in the co-creation process to the customer, who should control the creation and delivery of the value.

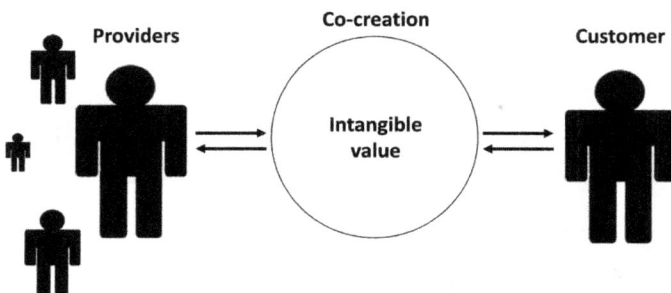

Figure 1.4 Value in-context model

Finally, three decades ago, Pine and Gilmore (1999) introduced what was then an emerging economic system, termed the *experience economy*, which describes a new way to connect with customers and increase their satisfaction and loyalty. They claimed that services are like commodities and that the experience economy is built on the service economy that, in turn, is built on the goods economy. In addition, they argued that while the goods economy entails the exchange of tangible value from producer to consumer and the service economy is based on the co-creation of intangible value by provider and customer, the experience economy is driven by memorable value, the creation of which requires a person or business to stage the experience and a guest, the customer, who participates in and perceives it.

Sustainability

During the shift to a more service oriented conceptualization of human societies, environmental catastrophes in the forms of air, water, and ground pollution as well as climate changes and loss of biodiversity became parts of our daily lives. Additionally, the influences of human actions on the environment, for better or for worse, and the fact that environmental issues disregard borders and do not distinguish between race, sex, or religion, were acknowledged. But the prevailing models of environmental *conservation* and *preservation* at the time (Allen 1980), which sought to maintain the ecosystem in its present form, addressed the implications for the environment of economic and social activities and conceptualized environmental awareness and action as completely separate issues. These approaches were therefore replaced by more proactive, integrative, and future-oriented models of *environmental protection* (O'Riordan 1995). Likewise, basic research into and knowledge of *ecology*, which investigates the interactions between organisms and their environment (Odum, Odum, and Andrews 1971), were broadened and deepened. In addition, at the same time, a variety of green political movements and ecological, nongovernmental organizations began to appear around the world. Collectively, these initiatives aimed to replace end-of-the-pipe solutions by focusing on rational resource use and pollution prevention rather than on treatment, and by implementing cleaner production methods, for example, *green chemistry* and *engineering, eco-fashion, green building,* etc. In addition, as the product dominant logic is based on the manufacture of goods, over the years a variety of *clean technologies,* or *Clean Techs* (Pernick and Wilder 2007), which seek to streamline production with respect to resource use and to reduce the output of by-products and pollution, were developed and implemented. Although the above-mentioned frameworks devised to protect the environment yielded greener or more environmentally friendly products, they neither effected real change in the awareness or action of most consumers nor halted the destructive effects of the consumption culture. The subsequent need to integrate environmental, social, and economic elements in a single model led to the emergence of the new paradigm of *sustainability* (Edwards 2005; Dresner 2008).

Sustainability is the capacity of ecosystems to bear the stress of economic and social processes while meeting not only the needs of the present generation, but also those of future generations and preserving enough physical space for subsequent generations to meet their own needs. It is thus mainly based on broad and comprehensive daily decision-making processes that integrate economic-, social-, and environmental-values and also on the rational use of both physical and nonphysical natural resources. As such, the quest for sustainability is the biggest challenge facing humanity today.

The pursuit of sustainability can be facilitated by shrinking the gap between humans and their natural world. Since the dawn of humanity—when people were hunter-gatherers who obtained all of their needs directly from nature, human history has taken us through the agricultural revolution, when manmade food was produced by the direct acquisition of resources from nature, through the industrial revolution that signaled a shift to the mass production of synthetic goods manufactured indirectly from nature, and finally, into the service revolution, the products of which comprise intangible values based on human resources—humans have become increasingly estranged from nature. But in fact, the pursuit of sustainability entails an opportunity to revitalize that vital connection: sustainability and service are mutually related, and as such, services can constitute the main channel through which sustainability is produced and delivered, and sustainability can be defined as a service performed by the current generation for subsequent generations.

CHAPTER 2

Sustainability and Service

The idea of sustainability, regularly evoked today to evaluate our behavior and how we make decisions (Dresner 2008; Edwards 2005), refers, in general, to a very old and simple concept known as the *Golden Rule*. A fundamental moral rule or ethic of reciprocity, the Golden Rule implores us to "treat others as you want to be treated," which in a nutshell, expresses the notion of sustainability. In their 1987 report entitled "Our Common Future", the Brundtland Commission from the United Nations World Commission on Environment and Development (WCED) simply defined sustainability as an action or a process that fulfills present and future needs together (Brundtland et al., 1987). Yet in more practical terms, sustainability concerns the integration and reconciliation of environmental, social, and economic values to maintain life in the long term.

The concept of sustainability can and must be applied to every process, product, city, and society, among others. Indeed, the shift from an industrial to a service economy has also been recognized as a potential opportunity to embed social and environmental values in the service sector (Wolfson et al., 2015). Moreover, as service systems are becoming more comprehensive, complex, and interdisciplinary (Fitzsimmons and Fitzsimmons 2006; Alter 2008), and the service dominant logic approach can help companies and organizations gain new insight into how to co-create values with their customers—by imbuing every service production, delivery, and use process with sustainability—new services that support and alter the sustainability of goods production, delivery, and use must also be added—a process that will inevitability promote substantial progress toward achieving global sustainability.

CleanServ

In 1992, the World Business Council for Sustainable Development (WBCSD) introduced the notion of *eco-efficiency* in an effort to offer a general model for the changes that must be adopted and implemented by humans to translate theory into action and reach the ultimate goal of sustainability. In general, eco-efficiency dictates that process design and development be based on the rational use of resources, the implementation of efficient and responsible operation modes, and the prevention or reduction of effluents and related discharges into the environment (World Business Council for Sustainable Development 2000; DeSimone and Popoff 2000). Although eco-efficiency was initially conceptualized in terms of manufacturing processes, different types of clean services (i.e., CleanServs) envisioned within the framework of the increasingly important service dominant logic also constitute a means for realizing some of the goals of eco-efficiency (Table 2.1) (Wolfson, Tavor, and Mark 2013a, 2014; Wolfson et al., 2015). Defined as service-based solutions that are competitive with, if not superior to, their conventional, tangible

Table 2.1 CleanServs categories and examples

Category	Description	Example
Prevention	Prevent the production of goods and provide the same solution with services instead	Using Bitcoin or bank transfer instead of cash money, check, or credit card
Reduction	Couple a service with a certain good, thereby reducing overall production of this good	Renting a dress instead of buying one
Replacing	Offer an alternative product-service system that provides the same solution	Traveling by bus or train instead of by taxi
Efficiency	Add a service that improves the utilization of resources and/or reduces discharges to the surroundings during the production, delivery or use of a certain good or service	Using *Moovit* application to improve access to and use of public transportation
Offset	Add a service that compensates for the amounts of resources utilized and/or discharged during the production, delivery, or use of a certain good or service	Using a bottle recycling service

or intangible counterparts, CleanServs prevent, reduce, replace, streamline (i.e., make efficienct), or offset the production of goods and services. In addition, CleanServs also increase the awareness, the responsibilities, and the actions of both provider and customer toward more efficient and sustainable service provision.

One of the routes by which physical resource utilization and the negative impacts of manufacturing on the social and natural environments can be reduced is to offer a solution that is based solely on services instead of goods (i.e., prevention CleanServ). Although this type of CleanServ is deemed superior to the other four in terms of its ability to promote sustainability, it is not always practical or applicable. In addition, because the production and delivery of services also entail the use of physical resources and undesirable discharge (e.g., pollutants) to the environment, the move from a solution based on physical resources to that based on nonphysical resources is justified only if it is eventually more sustainable.

Another widespread method to increase the efficiency of goods usage is by coupling it with a service in a *product-service system*. Product-service systems are "marketable systems of products and services capable of fulfilling a user's demand" (Goedkoop et al., 1999). Tukker suggested that product-service systems can be categorized into eight types ranging from 'pure product' to 'pure service' (Tukker 2004) that, in turn, can be divided into three different groups: (1) product-based—the product is dominant, (2) service-based—the service is dominant, and (3) solution-based—the product and the service contribute equally to the solution in a unique combination (Wolfson et al., 2015). Finally, the fact that the *servicizing* of products usually entails not only an economic benefit, but also an environmental one in the form of a smaller impact on the environment, has led to a corresponding change in terminology such that product-service systems are referred to as *eco-efficient services* (Brezet et al., 2001). Moreover, because the use of eco-efficient services usually leads to reductions in the amounts of goods that need to be produced to perform the service by promoting more efficient and extended use of each item (e.g., renting, leasing, or sharing of goods), they therefore present cleaner solutions (i.e., CleanServs of the reduction type). For example, carpooling, a simple example of a reduction type CleanServ, reduces the number of cars on the road (and the associated pollution) by grouping people who have similar travel times and destinations in a single car instead of each person driving his or her own car.

The shift in emphasis from goods to services can also be realized by exploiting CleanServs of the replacement type, in which alternative couplings of goods and services generate the same solutions as in the past, but with reduced negative impacts on the environment. For example, changing entertainment consumption habits to favor streaming movies on the Internet as opposed to purchasing DVD copies of the films allows people to enjoy the same movies while eliminating the need to produce the discs, which also leads to reductions in the associated packaging, storage, and distribution. Finally, the sustainability of production and delivery processes, in terms of goods or services, can be improved by adding supporting and complementary services that streamline the solution (i.e., CleanServs of the efficiency type), or that compensate for the less efficient use of resources or the discharge of by-products entailed in those processes (i.e., CleanServs of the offset type). In this respect, *environmental services* that incorporate combinations of scientific, technical, management, and advisory activities aimed at minimizing natural resource use and environmental damage, for example, services that promote the recycling of resources, and *green services*, which incorporate and promote more efficient resource use and reduce environmental impacts during their provision, can be employed (Wolfson 2015).

To explore the options offered by CleanServs, the example of the book market is discussed. From forest harvesting, to paper production, to book disposal, book production has a heavy environmental impact that is associated with high utilization of energy and water, and subsequent emissions of greenhouse gases and effluents. Though books can be borrowed from a library (i.e., CleanServs of the reduction type) or downloaded electronically via the Internet using different electronic devices (i.e., CleanServs of the replacement type), many people still prefer to hold the hard copy in their hands and to own the book or to give it as a present. Thus, using an efficiency type CleanServ, for example, by managing the production more efficiently and reducing the numbers of printed books that are unsold or by using more effective shipping and distribution systems, can reduce the environmental impact of the book's value chain. Furthermore, using recycled paper in the production process (i.e., CleanServ of offset type) can reduce both tree harvesting and the disposal of paper in landfills. Finally, second-hand book shops constitute a service that can help fulfill people's desire to own hard copies, which simultaneously can be used for unlimited amounts of time, can reduce the production of new books and the disposal or recycling of used books. Insofar as the second-hand book service is associated with decreases in physical resource utilization and in discharges of pollution to the surroundings, it can be defined as a Clean-Serv of reduction type.

Sustainable Service Model

To put sustainability into practice and generate *sustainable services* will require more than merely implementing efficient physical resource management in the production, delivery, and use of service. First and foremost, sustainable service is that which fulfills customer needs and can be perpetuated for long periods of time without negatively influencing the customer's natural or social environment (Wolfson et al., 2010; Wolfson, Tavor, and Mark 2013b). Based both on the smart and efficient integration of physical and nonphysical resources and on behaving with environmental and social awareness, sustainable services also entail substantial economic benefits. In addition, sustainable services take into account their potential short and long-term effects, on both the local and the global scales, and they are necessarily inclusive, involving individuals as well as societies. Finally, sustainable services also incorporate a novel perspective on the relationships between customers, providers, and suppliers, and they reconfigure the relationship between products and services (Figure 2.1).

The fundamentals of sustainable service and the strategies for making a service more sustainable are still in development. As stated earlier, (Elkington 2004), the main challenge is to advance beyond the mere realization of eco-efficient products and processes toward achieving "*triple bottom line*" solutions that include social and environmental dimensions with the economic measures traditionally evaluated in bottom line assessments of performance.

Wolfson et al., (2010) recently presented a novel perspective on sustainability together with a model that describes the relationship between sustainability and service within the framework of service science. In that

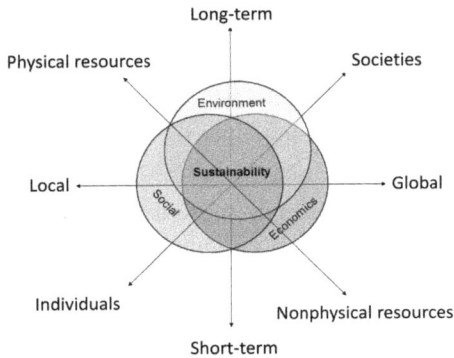

Figure 2.1 Components of sustainable service

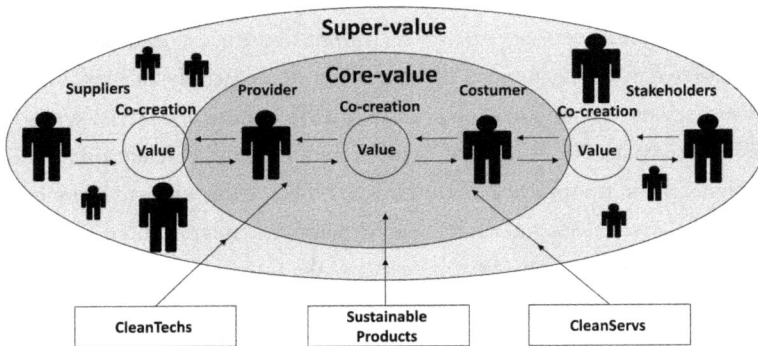

Figure 2.2 Sustainable service

work, sustainable service is defined not only as a service that fulfills customer demands, but also minimally impacts both the natural and the social environments. In addition, a sustainable service must incorporate sustainability as a basic value and essential part of each service. The model therefore suggests that a sustainable service should imbue each phase of the service value chain with sustainability (Figure 2.2) while considering all stakeholders, from today's suppliers to the generations of tomorrow. It should also engender a fundamental shift in the traditional roles of the primary participants in the service. Thus, the service supplier becomes a provider, and the consumer assumes the role of customer. These new roles are defined by a value co-creation process, in which value is produced and used jointly and reciprocally by the provider and the customer.

The value co-creation process integral to the new model proposes that each value chain should be seen as a combination of a *core-value*, or the essence of the solution that a certain service provides and that should be co-created and delivered from a provider to a customer, and a *super-value*, or the generation of other, supporting and complementary values, via additional direct and indirect suppliers and customers (Figure 2.2). Simply put, the value chain of a sustainable service is initiated by suppliers who co-create the super-value with the provider, who then co-cerates the core-value with the customer while simultaneously considering the co-creation of super-value with other stakeholders, which include subsequent generations. In this model, all value production and delivery stages are based on the rational use of resources and on the efficient utilization of sustainable products, CleanTechs, and CleanServs. Furthermore, in addition to mitigating environmental risks and harms, sustainable services will also generate tangible benefits. Finally, the new perspective and model should also serve as a framework for entrepreneurship and innovation in the research and practice of both service and sustainability while generating new and alternative values and supplying customer demands more sustainably.

Insofar as services are not stand-alone entities and they interact with other values and processes to achieve the service goal, it is also imperative that sustainable service design be integrated with other services, and manufacturing, agricultural, and mining processes. To that end, Wolfson et al., proposed a new model, termed "S^3—sustainability as service science model", which describes sustainable service as the integration of physical and nonphysical resources, and tangible and intangible values (Figure 2.3). Thus, the model of sustainable service comprises two main stages: first, a sustainable decision is made by a service, where the decision relies on the service's resources, including natural resources, technologies, and information and knowledge; second, the most sustainable choice is selected from among the alternatives after evaluating each in terms of its integration of services, and manufacturing and agricultural processes (Wolfson et al., 2010).

Service axis

Customer → Supplier   Service values   Supplier → Customer

Future oriented

Technologies   Environment   Manufacture   Environment

Natural
Resources   Sustainable
Decision   Service   Sustainable
Choice

Information
Knowledge   Agriculture

Implementation

Time axis
Past   Present   Future $n \to \infty$

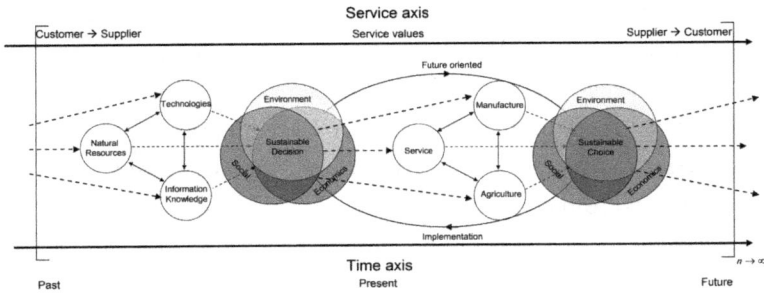

Figure 2.3 S^3—Sustainability as service science model (Wolfson et al., 2010)

In contrast to manufacturing and agricultural processes, joint and reciprocal value co-creation constitutes a fundamental prerequisite of a service, and therefore, sustainability should also be an integral part of the interactions among providers and beneficiaries. This means that the provider-customer relationship must advance beyond simply sharing the responsibilities for the physical and nonphysical resources (e.g., knowledge, skills, efforts, and capabilities) to include a sustainable division between provider and customer of all resources and tasks associated with the service. From this perspective, the decision of which service mode to choose (e.g., *self-service* or *e-service*) is also important. For example, withdrawing money from a bank can be done in a self-service fashion using an ATM, eliminating the need to physically visit a teller at a bank, which requires significantly more facilities and resources. Likewise, bills can be paid using an e-service for a more sustainable alternative to driving to the post office or to the bank.

Achieving the goal of sustainable service can also be promoted by adopting a natural mimicry approach, which entails designing service systems based on the so-called rules of nature (Wolfson, Tavor, and Mark 2011). Simply put, these rules promote the rational use of resources, energy efficiency, adoption of future-oriented and life cycle perspectives, and the ability to adapt smoothly to changes in an evolutionary fashion. In addition, because the production of goods is inherently tied to natural resource use and associated with the discharge to the environment of various by-products, the production and delivery of a solution based on an intangible value (i.e., service) is preferred from the perspective of sustainability.

Sustainability as Service

Sustainability itself is an intangible value that is produced and delivered simultaneously (i.e., it is inseparable), that can neither be stored nor returned (i.e., it is not perishable), and whose overall appearance or performance depends on the time and place of provision and on both the provider and the customer (i.e., it is heterogeneous). As such, it is in fact a service par excellence (Wolfson et al., 2015), and similar to a service, its intangibility and perishability refer to the fact that it cannot be seen, touched, or stored. Indeed, this is also one of the main reasons why it is so difficult to comprehend the meaning of sustainability and, more importantly, its implementation such a challenge.

Treating sustainability as a service, however, greatly simplifies the process and allows the philosophy and ideas behind sustainability to be put into practice (e.g., methods, tools, etc.) while simultaneously defining it more clearly and concretely. Primarily, approaching sustainability as a service dictates that the provider/providers, the customer/customers, and the value be clearly specified and that actions be taken to gain insight into the components of the value chain. It also obliges the provider to design and develop a value that can be delivered and eventually used by the customer. In addition, it encourages the formation of a value co-creation process between the provider and the customer built on the efficient use of both physical and nonphysical resources and the correct division of those resources between the two actors. In the long term framework of sustainability, the customer is eventually recruited to be a provider of sustainability to other stakeholders including those in the next generation. Finally, by defining sustainability as a service, both the idea and the practice of sustainability can be advanced.

For the design, development, production, and implementation of sustainable services, Wolfson et al., (2015) suggested the following seven principles:

1. **Sustainable value:** Sustainability should be an essential part of value delivery (i.e., triple bottom line).
2. **Whole-value orientation:** Both core- and super-values should be considered.

3. **Value co-creation:** Value co-creation processes—in which the provider furnishes a platform to deliver the service and the customer participates in the service delivery by sharing some of the resources, tasks, and capabilities—should be included.
4. **Value continuity:** The customer should be allowed, and even compelled, to become a provider of sustainability (i.e., from customer to provider).
5. **Value life cycle:** All phases of the service life cycle, including both physical and nonphysical resources, should incorporate sustainability.
6. **Intangibility of value:** The preferred solution should be based on an intangible value and not on a tangible product (i.e., CleanServs).
7. **Sustainability as value:** Sustainability should be delivered as a service in and of itself.

Outline for Making a Service Sustainable

In the assessment of a service that begins any effort to improve the service's sustainability, the main issues to address include the motivation behind the improvement effort, the identity of who should initiate and enable sustainability, and a clarification of how the service can be made more sustainable. The drivers that motivate providers and/or customers to adopt sustainability practices are highly complex, and they vary within and between the two groups. In some cases, environmental consciousness and true concern for the natural and social environments constitute the motivation of the providers and/or the customers to act more sustainably and choose more sustainable routes. In other cases, the process is motivated by regulations, such as the prohibition on discharging different types of effluents or wastes into the environment. Additionally, sustainability of services can also be considered in the context of value constellations with other stakeholders, including government, suppliers, and indirect customers. Furthermore, in financial terms, efforts to imbue services with sustainability by increasing the efficiency and/or productivity of the service can not only improve customer satisfaction and loyalty, but usually also increase financial profits—a central incentive driving the traditional business model. Likewise, monetary incentives can be offered to producers to adopt environmentally sustainable practices. For example, the main incentive behind the participation of people in a plastic recycling program is probably environmental concern. Yet a regulation that requires suppliers to collect their empty packaging after customer consumption or a system that charges a deposit on cans and bottles can also encourage people to recycle. Finally, creating values based on easier and more flexible options (e.g., e-governance services), may also simultaneously increase the sustainability of the solution

As stated, sustainability can be initiated and introduced into the service production, delivery, and use processes by the provider, by the customer, or as a joint endeavor. The effect of increasing the service sustainability of only the provider while the customer plays no active role will usually be limited to resource utilization and facilities, and technology usage in the production or delivery stages of the service. In this respect, the provider can also encourage his or her suppliers to be more sustainable. Moreover, if necessary, in the event that the suppliers resist the call to increase their sustainability, the provider can even compel them to do so by, for example, linking their business agreement to the sustainability prerequisite. Likewise, providers can recruit their customers to behave more sustainably by enabling sustainability during the service delivery process, but this route requires some degree of customer participation for it to function. On the other hand, the customer can also initiate sustainability by using the service in a sustainable manner and by requesting that the provider adopt more sustainable practices. Finally, among the preferred methods to introduce sustainability to a service is through the value co-creation process, which entails, among other actions, that the resources and tasks associated with the service be split between provider and customer. Likewise, the sustainability of each service provision can be improved by efficiently managing both the physical and nonphysical resources (e.g., materials and energy, facilities, effort, and information and knowledge) necessary to perform the service.

To make a service more sustainable, the following evaluative steps should be taken:

1. Reduce the service value chain to its fundamental components:
   a. Identify the core-value (i.e., the purpose of the service).
   b. Identify the provider and the customer.

   c. Identify and characterize the main steps and technologies involved in the production and delivery of the service from the provider to the customer and the manner in which it is used by the customer.
   d. Identify and characterize the suppliers, supplies, and indirect customers as well as other stakeholders.
   e. Identify the super-value (i.e., values that are associated with or that support the core-value).
   f. Identify the map of resources and capabilities and determine how they differ between the provider and the customer.
   g. Identify the economic, social, and environmental values of the service.
   h. Identify the responsibilities of each actor in the production, delivery, and use of the service to sustainability.
2. Assess the service:
   a. Qualify and quantify the utilization of physical and nonphysical resources: materials and energy, facilities, effort, and information and knowledge.
   b. Identify the short- and long-term effects and the local and global impacts of the service.
   c. Qualify and quantify the division of resources and tasks between the provider and the customer, and between the core- and super-values.
3. Search for alternatives:
   a. Identify alternative routes to supply the same solution.
   b. Identify supportive services to increase the sustainability of the core-service.
   c. Compare between alternatives based on all the above-mentioned points (e.g., resources, values).

Example

Medical consultation with a doctor is a common, relatively simple service based on a two-way social interaction between doctor and patient that is used daily by many people. According to the outline above, the service is characterized as follows:

   a. Core-value: medical advice.
   b. Provider and customer: doctor and patient.

Table 2.2 Division of resources and capabilities in the service of medical consulting

	Value	Provider	Customer
Material and energy	Core	None	None
	Super	Electricity, water, manpower, etc.	Gasoline (to reach the clinic)
Facilities	Core	Medical equipment	None
	Super	Office, computer, clinic equipment	Car
Effort	Core	Time	Time
	Super	Studying and continuing education program	None
Information and knowledge	Core	Medical studies, continuing education program	None
	Super	Medical studies, continuing education program	None

   c. Main steps in the value chain are: (1) arrival at the clinic, (2) discussion, (3) examination, (4) documentation, and (5) treatment.

   d. Main suppliers and supplies: hospital or medical clinic. Indirect customers as well as other stakeholders: the patient's family members and the insurance company.

   e. Super-value: running the facilities and reaching the clinic.

   f. The map of resources and capabilities and how they differ between the provider and the customer are illustrated in Table 2.2.

The subsequent steps of identifying the environmental, social, and economic values of the service and of assessing and evaluating the service while searching for alternative routes to perform the same service will be discussed in the following chapters.

CHAPTER 3

Evaluating Sustainable Services

The word 'value' has a variety of meanings, from magnitude or quantity, to worth or importance, to the moral and ethical precepts on which we base our behavior. Values are also integrally connected with culture, education, and experience, and therefore, they also depend on the place and time when they are delivered. Finally, values do not stand alone, and in fact, they are usually a part of a set of values or a *value-system* that guides people's behavioral preferences in all situations.

Product Value

What is the value of air? Its exchange-value is zero, as it is freely available, while its use-value is inestimable and actually infinite, as it gives and sustains life. Yet, though we do not have to produce or deliver air, deforestation that affects the natural life cycle of oxygen, thereby reducing the amount of oxygen produced, on the one hand, and air pollution that reduces the quality of air, on the other hand, can be quantified and translated into monetary values.

In contrast, water, which is also essential for life, has a monetary value or price that reflects the resources used during its production (e.g., drawing or desalination, purification, and delivery and distribution) and, in the later stages of its life cycle, during wastewater treatment and recycling. However, water's exchange-value is far lower than its use-value, the former of which does not account for the effects of water pumping on the condition and the quality of water resources (e.g., aquifer or river) or on the ability to continue pumping water. Moreover, the exchange-value does not include the effects the production and use of water have on ecosystem functions or on biodiversity (i.e., *environmental-value*). It also does not weigh the effects on the social and natural environments of wastewater that is discarded at the end of the water life cycle.

In addition, water also has a *social-value*, and water security—which refers to a supply of water in suitable quantities and of acceptable quality to support human health and livelihoods—is a fundamental right of every human being. Water security, which depends critically on who is in control of the water sources, is one of the main prerequisites for a flourishing society, on the one hand, but on the other hand, it also engenders power struggles and wars around the world. Thus, in the context of sustainability, the measures that define the value of a product, in terms of goods or services, should be defined in a broader fashion that considers direct and indirect values.

In this respect, a direct value relates both to the direct utilization of resources in the production and delivery of the value together with the direct use of the product. An indirect value, by contrast, is attributed to the effect of the product's life cycle on the social and natural environments, and on nature capital. In addition, it refers to the indirect utilization of ecosystem services and the ability of nature to preserve ecosystems so that they can continue to provide these services in the future.

As noted in the previous chapter, the World Business Council for Sustainable Development (WBCSD) offered the concept of eco-efficiency as a tool to foster sustainable development (World Business Council for Sustainable Development 2000). In so doing, the WBCSD stated that eco-efficiency can be achieved "by the delivery of competitively priced goods and services that satisfy human needs and bring quality of life while progressively reducing environmental impacts of goods and resource intensity throughout the entire life cycle to a level at least in line with the earth's estimated carrying capacity". Since then, various eco-efficiency measures that quantify environmental impacts while increasing environmental value have been introduced (Huppes and Ishikawa 2007). These include *environmental productivity*, which is the ratio between the added value of a product to the added environmental impact of the whole life cycle of the product.

Sustainability Measures

One of the methods used to evaluate the value of a product and to imbue planning and decision-making processes with sustainability as a policy tool is by performing a sustainability assessment. It allows the environmental, social, and economic impacts of a process or a product to be quantified while situating them on a unified, comparative scale. Additionally, it helps increase the performance, competitiveness, and profitability of each value and it adds extra values. Moreover, it allows the sustainability values of competing alternatives to be compared on the same basis (Kloepffer 2008; Pope, Annandale, and Morrison-Saunders 2004; Singh et al., 2009).

A typical sustainability assessment should begin by precisely defining a system and its boundaries, such as a good, a service, a city, or a country. Once the system and its boundaries have been defined, the different inputs and outputs (e.g., materials, energy, manpower, etc.) as well as their effects on social and environmental livability and on the economy should be considered. However, there is still some disagreement about how to define system boundaries with respect to a sustainability assessment and about what measures can be used to quantitatively represent the sustainability of a process, a good, or a service.

Generally speaking, measures can be used to understand or monitor a certain property, phenomenon, or situation, and in the process, indicating its current status and how far it is from a target status. They can also provide important guidance about prospective actions that can be taken to achieve the desired target, and they can even be designed to warn people of a current or impending problem. Finally, measures are also useful for comparing different systems or values.

Because by definition, sustainability practices must not only account for but also integrate environmental, social, and economic aspects, the measure of sustainability should consider indicators from each of these realms that correspond to a creation value and situation, indexes that integrate those indicators and that account for the relative importance of each, and measures that contain indicators and indexes from various fields. However, despite the variety of sustainability indicators, indexes, and measures that have been offered and used over the last decade, efforts to combine all the aspects of sustainability into a single, comparative number are ongoing. In addition, not all measures are suitable for every system, be it country, city, goods, or services. Furthermore, some measures have strong impacts and are highly sensitive in one case while in others they have almost no effect whatsoever.

In general, each indicator is used to assess and quantify a certain property, and as such, it is usually narrow and specific (e.g., the temperature or weight of a system, or the amount of energy that was used in a process), and can be easily measured by using simple means. Table 3.1 summarizes several representative indicators in the environmental, social, and economic realms. Insofar as these indicators are general, they are applicable in most sustainability assessments.

Environmental indicators usually measure the amounts of natural resources that were used during a process or applied to a system, and the amount of discharge to the environment during the production or use processes and at the end of the life of the system. Examples include the amount of water used in a process or per product and the amount of wastewater that was drained to the environment in the same process. And in many cases, even these relatively simple indicators can be broken down into more fundamental measures. Thus, the indicator of the total water usage associated with a process can also specify the amount or share of gray water—recycled water from households or residential buildings that is free of fecal contamination—used in that process and the percentage of wastewater generated by the process that was treated and returned to the system. Other environmental indicators, such as the emission levels of air pollutants like carbon monoxide, particle pollution, and volatile organic compounds (VOC), or the amount of hazardous waste, help quantify the impact of the process or the system on the environment.

Social indicators, which measure social development or quality of life in terms of people or whole societies, usually cover a broad range of fields, including demographic variables, education, health, housing, and the labor market, among others. Some typical social indicators are population size, growth, and composition, life expectancy, poverty and income levels, and unemployment rates (Table 3.1). The last group of

Table 3.1 Representative sustainability indicators and indexes

Indicator/index	Explanation
Environmental indicators	
Emission of pollutant (particles, nitrogen oxides, sulfur oxides, carbon monoxide, ozone, etc.)	Amount of pollutant per unit time or per volume of air
Release of metals to water (Lead, mercury, cadmium, etc.)	Amount of pollutant per volume of water
Use intensity of resources (water, forest, energy, etc.)	Amount of resource use per capita, per time or per area
Waste generation	Amount of waste per capita or per area
Resource recycling (wastewater, waste, etc.)	Amount (or percentage) of recycled resource per capita or per area
Environmental indexes	
Carbon footprint	Total greenhouse gas emissions of a process
Air quality	Air quality relative to the requirements of one or more biotic species
Social indicators	
Household income	Combined incomes of all people sharing a particular household or place of residence
Life expectancy	Measure of how long the average person lives
Poverty level	Number of people (in a given age group) whose income falls below the poverty line
Health expenditure	Sum of public and private health spending
Social indexes	
Human development index	Measure of a country's level of human development
Social progress index	Extent to which a country provides for the social needs of its citizens
Economic indicators	
Unemployment rate	Percentage of the total labor force that is unemployed
Industrial production	Output of the industrial sector of the economy
Balance of trade	Difference between a country's imports and exports
Retail trade	Functions and activities involved in the selling of commodities directly to consumers
Hourly earning	Average hourly wages of all employees
Economic indexes	
Gross domestic product	Measure of a country's economic performance
Consumer price index	Changes in the price level of a market basket of consumer goods and services purchased by households

indicators, the economic indicators, informs about the financial state, activity or performance of a system and includes, for instance, the price of a product, the average number of employee work hours per week, the exchange rate, and international trade measures. Finally, note that some indicators are applicable in multiple fields. For example, energy consumption can be used to express a system's sustainability in environmental and economic terms, and income can be both a social and an economic indicator.

In contrast to indicators, which are narrow and specific by definition, indexes are derived from indicators, and as such, they convey more information. Moreover, the knowledge required in the selection process to determine which indicators are suitable for a particular index and how to correctly combine them is greater than that needed to devise indicators. Lastly, indexes can be based on the integration of indicators from one, two, or all three fields. Their combinatorial nature, however, affords them a level of complexity that renders indexes less straightforward conceptually than indicators.

A popular example of an environmental index is that of air quality (sometimes referred to as the air pollution index), which is a generalized way to describe the quality of the air we breathe and its associated level of health risk to humans. This index, which accounts for several major air pollutants, such as ground-level ozone, particulate matter, carbon monoxide, sulfur dioxide, and nitrogen dioxide, is expressed on a numerical continuum on which the higher the number, the greater the risk to human health. In addition, the numerical range of the scale is further divided into four basic levels of health risk (low, moderate, high, and very high) that are represented by different colors. However, the range of the scale, the color coding system used to express the different levels of air quality, and air quality definitions (i.e., the measures used to indicate air quality) vary from country to country.

Social and economic indexes are intricately linked with environmental indexes. A principal social index is the human development index (HDI), which is an expression of average levels in key dimensions of human development, (i.e., quality of life and life expectancy education level, and standard of living). HDI is applicable both to large-scale, inter-country comparisons and to small-scale comparisons that examine, for example, the conditions and educational levels of employees in different factories. Lastly, one of the most widely used economic indexes is the gross domestic product (GDP), which calculates the monetary value of all the goods and services produced within a country's borders within a specific time period.

Numerous sustainability measures that comprise mixtures of environmental, social, and economic indicators and indexes such as ecological footprint, EcoTime and Bee-Factor have been introduced over the years. Already proposed in 1998, the ecological footprint is a measure of the area of productive land required to supply human demands and to absorb the impact of human activity on nature (Wackernagel and Rees 1998). The ecological footprint is calculated by summing the total area of cropland, grazing land, forest, and fishing grounds required to produce the energy, food, fiber, and synthetic products used by humans, used for housing and infrastructure as well as for leisure activities, and used to absorb the corresponding waste and polluting emissions. Although, traditionally, the ecological footprint was used to compare countries, today everyone can calculate his or her individual footprint by using calculators available on the Internet.

In the wake of the general acceptance of the ecological footprint as a viable index, other combinations of sustainability measures have been proposed. EcoTime translates the impacts of human activities on natural resource utilization at a certain location or in a defined time frame into a simple and intuitive number that can be easily grasped by most people (Shepon et al., 2013). Another example is the Bee-Factor, a dimensionless cost effectiveness or cost-benefit measure that is used to compare the sustainability of two alternative products or processes when the data to calculate the sustainability of each system or process alone is incomplete (Wolfson et al., 2015). Expressed by the ratio of the sustainability difference to the cost difference between the two alternatives, Bee-Factor represents the influence that one's choice can have on global sustainability.

However, the design of sustainability measures is not just about integrating the traditionally important features of the environmental, social, and economic realms, or about how to combine those realms in different proportions in the final measure, it is also about developing and calculating completely new measures. It starts with the conceptualization of novel indicators to measure the causes of environment damage instead of the damage itself. For example, the use and generation of toxic materials can be evaluated instead of merely assessing pollution levels. Likewise, the proportion of a product that can be repaired, re-used, or recycled can be examined in addition to measuring the amount of solid waste that is generated over the product life cycle. Recent years, therefore, have witnessed the proposal of some new sustainability indexes (Table 3.2) (van den Bergh and Antal 2014).

In addition to improving efficiency, sustainability measures can also be used to compare services. The carbon footprint, a measure of the greenhouse gas emissions over the course of the entire value chain of a product, is one of the most widely used sustainability measures. Carbon footprint is based on the energies and materials used over the product's life cycle, from the mining and extraction of the raw materials to the end of the product's life. However, despite the applicability of a unified comparative scale, like the carbon footprint, to comparisons of multiple products simultaneously, the application of such scales in the assessment of services is not as widespread as with goods—an outcome that may be due, in part, to the difficulty of clearly defining the boundaries of a service to calculate its carbon footprint. Table 3.3 illustrates the carbon footprint

Table 3.2 New sustainability measures

Measure	Explanation	Based on
Measures of Economic Welfare (MEW)	Consumption and investment items that contribute directly to economic well-being	Gross domestic product, environmental and social impacts and damage
Index of Sustainable Economic Welfare (ISEW)	Services that directly influence human welfare or the benefits of economic activity	Gross domestic product, environmental and social impacts and damage
Genuine Progress Indicator (GPI)	Nation's genuine overall economic and social well-being in term of sustainable progress	Gross domestic product, environmental and social impacts and damage
Happy Planet Index (HPI)	Sustainability of people's well-being, or the ecological efficiency with which high quality of life is achieved	Life expectancy, experienced well-being, ecological footprint

Table 3.3 Carbon footprint of representative services

Service	CO_2eq footprint (g)	Main causes
Email[1]	4	Manufacturing & running the computer, the server, and the routers
Email with a large attachment[1]	50	Manufacturing & running the computer, the server, and the routers
Short-haul flights[2]	360 (per passenger per kilometer)	Fuel, airplane maintenance and manufacturing
Downloading digital music[3]	45 (per CD)	Energy used to run data centers
Single outpatient appointment in hospital[4]	50	Running equipment and facilities
Sending a letter by direct mail[5]	20	Running equipment and facilities

[1] Berners-Lee 2015.
[2] Ross 2009.
[3] Weber, Koomey and Matthews 2009.
[4] NHS 2010.
[5] Pitney Bowes Inc. 2008.

of some representative services and the main activities and resources upon which the index is based.

Sustainable Service Measures

Wolfson et al., (2015) offered some new measures to calculate the sustainability levels of services (Table 3.4) by using the value chain analysis introduced in Chapter 2. These measures are based on the *sustainability number* (SN) of the whole service, which is calculated by aggregating indicators and indexes from the environmental, social, and economic realms.

Transportation Services—an Example

As previously stated, the indicators and indexes that should be used to assess and calculate the sustainability of each system or process differ from one another. Dependent primarily on the nature and the defining

Table 3.4 Measures for the sustainability of services

Measure	Definition	Calculation
Sustainability level of co-creation	Division in responsibilities between the provider and the customer for the resources and tasks associated with the service	$\dfrac{SN - customer}{SN - provider}$
Sustainability value-ratio	Split between the core-value and the super-value in terms of resources and tasks	$\dfrac{SN - Core\text{-}value}{SN - Super\text{-}value}$
Sustainability impact factor	Impact of an individual value chain building block on the sustainability of the whole service	$\dfrac{(SN)i}{\Sigma(SN)i}$

characteristics of each system, they should reflect as accurately as possible the impact that the system has on the social and natural environments. The first step of the assessment process, therefore, should aim to identify the most relevant and representative indicators from among those for which sufficient data exist to enable their calculation. Moreover, it is also important to choose indicators that are both flexible and sensitive to changes.

The question about which sustainability indicators should be applied in the evaluation and planning of transport solutions has occupied many of the direct stakeholders in the transportation sector as well as urban planners and researches (Litman 2007). Today it is clear that to be sustainable, transportation solutions must integrate elements from the social, economic, and environmental realms, and they must be designed for the service needs of different sectors and groups. Yet a sustainable transportation solution should first of all incorporate sustainability as an integral part of its overall goal. Moreover, the sustainability measures that reflect such considerations should be defined and calculated at all stages of the development process—from its planning stage to its implementation and subsequent operation.

The core-value of transportation, which is the transport of passengers, should be realized via a service that is efficient (rapid and punctual) and that can be delivered with minimum costs (i.e., to the passengers, society, etc.) and maximum reliability, flexibility, accessibility, and safety.

However, to achieve the goal of a sustainable public transportation service, social values like equity and environmental values that promote reductions in energy consumption and air pollution emissions should also be added to the core-value. Moreover, a sustainable transportation system should offer diverse transportation solutions, such as bus, metro, and bicycle as well as walking and carpooling, each of which can be used alone or in combinations of two or more on any given journey.

To ensure that such varied transportation solutions are comfortable for people to use, they must be designed with smart pricing and payment systems that will allow and even encourage customers to simply, smartly, and cost-effectively exploit combinations between the different means of transport as a super-value. The means to achieve these goals and promote a sustainable journey can involve, for example, linking train and bus schedules so that customers can rely on their train arrival time to coincide with a bus departure from the same station and installing bicycle parking facilities and a bicycle rental service at the station.

As a direct stakeholder in the process of developing a sustainable transportation solution, the transportation service provider also has an important role to play, and it is in the provider's interest to increase the efficiency of each ride and to help create a sustainable super-value. To that end, transportation service providers have at their disposal a variety of means that can be exploited, including the use of smart schedules and lane management to increase the satisfaction and loyalty of its customers, and the optimization of vehicle size to the anticipated number of passengers for each journey. Thus, while a full-size bus will be needed during the morning and evening rush hours to serve the large numbers of people simultaneously traveling to and from work, during off-peak hours, the provider can use a small minibus. Furthermore, the bus company can publish online bus information at the station, on its Internet site, or by different software applications, thereby assisting their customers in route planning and balancing the number of passengers per journey. However, the customer can also increase the sustainability of a transportation service, primarily by efficiently co-creating the service and using the bus alone or in conjunction with other transportation means instead of resorting to the use of a private car, but also by sharing information with the bus company's software application so that it will aid other passengers in the co-creation of the service value.

As mentioned earlier, the selection of transportation indicators should be based on several principles (Litman 2007). Firstly, the indicators should be comprehensive and cover various economic, social, and environmental impacts. In addition, data collection should be relatively easy and cost-effective, and the data should be accurate and presented in a way that enables alternatives to be compared on a single scale. Furthermore, the selected measures should be understandable and manageable to allow both the provider and the customer to make the best decisions.

Table 3.5, a summary of some of the main indicators for sustainable transportation services, was compiled from a survey of works in the field that were carried out worldwide.

As stated above, the main challenge associated with measuring the sustainability of a service is in the integration of the various indicators, which usually have different magnitudes and are expressed in different units, and the weighing of these indicators based on their relative impacts. For example, the presentation of renewable energy use in units of MJ/min renders that measure incompatible with either user rating percentage or transportation cost. However, this problem can generally be circumvented by converting all the indicators into a single unit, for example, monetary value, or by calculating dimensionless indicators. That, in turn, entails determining how to weigh the various indicators and the relative influences of energy use versus user satisfaction. Another approach is to decide based on the use of some of the indicators or indexes without combining them into one representative number. In addition, even a calculation of the environmental index associated with the creation of a transportation service is not straightforward, as it should integrate a variety of indicators, such as emissions of air pollutants and greenhouse gases, and noise pollution.

The concepts and the novel measurements offered above are illustrated with a study by Chester and Arpad (2009), who performed an environmental assessment of passenger transportation based on energy use or greenhouse gas emissions (i.e., carbon footprint) per passenger-kilometer-traveled (PKT). The study compared transportation modes, such as private car, bus, rail, and airplane, and included among

Table 3.5 Representative sustainable transportation indicators

Theme	Indicator
Environmental	
Climate change	Emissions of CO_2eq per capita per km
Air pollution	Emissions of air pollutants (CO, VOC, NOx, particulates, etc.) per capita per km
Noise pollution	Portion of population exposed to high levels of traffic noise
Land use	Land devoted to transportation facilities per capita
Renewable energy use	Percentage of renewable energy from total energy use
Social	
Transport activity	Total motorized movement of people or passenger-kilometers per GDP
Affordability	Portion of lower income household budgets spent on transport
Safety	Index of incidence of road injuries and fatalities
User rating	Users' overall level of satisfaction with transport system
Economic	
Cost efficiency	Transportation costs as a portion of total economic activity and per unit of GDP
Commute time	Average door-to-door commute travel time
Transport diversity	Variety and quality of transport options available in a community

the variables examined were operational components that can be assigned to the service's core-value (e.g., running the vehicle and idling time) and non-operational components that can be assigned to the service's super-value (e.g., vehicle manufacturing, maintenance, and insurance, infrastructure construction, operation and maintenance, and fuel production). Table 3.6 presents a comparison of the greenhouse gas emissions of light rail (in San Francisco) and of an urban diesel bus, both at peak and off-peak hours, with a carpooling service with four passengers. The emissions of each means of transportation were split into operational and non-operational emissions (i.e., core-value and super-value), and both the sustainability value-ratio and the sustainability level of co-creation were calculated.

As can be seen from the carbon footprint of each method of transportation, the total emissions of a light rail trip are approximately double those of an urban diesel bus trip at peak hours or of a carpool journey

Table 3.6 Greenhouse gas emissions of representative transportation services

	gCO_2 PKT			
	Light rail	Urban diesel bus (Peak)	Urban diesel bus (off-peak)	Carpool (4 people)
Operation core-value	43	38	305	36
Non-operation super-value	64	13	108	22.5
Total	107	51	413	58.5
Sustainability value-ratio	0.7	2.9	2.8	1.6
Sustainability level of co-creation	0.001–0.003	0.015–0.02	0.1–0.2	0.25

with four passengers. Moreover, the sustainability value-ratio of the light rail, which corresponds to the ratio of operational to non-operational emissions, indicates that most light rail emissions are attributed to non-operational components due to infrastructure construction and maintenance requirements. In the case of the urban diesel bus, however, emissions are attributed mainly to operational components, as reflected by the much higher sustainability value-ratio. In addition, while a trip in an urban bus filled to capacity during rush hour has half the emissions of the light rail, using the bus during off-peak hours, when it is used by fewer passengers, increases the emissions per passenger-kilometer-traveled (PKT) by eight-fold, resulting in much higher emissions compared to the light rail. Using a carpooling service, which of course immediately reduces the emissions per passenger-kilometer-traveled (PKT) of a trip in a private car, has an intermediate sustainability value-ratio between those of the light rail and the urban diesel bus.

The division in emissions between the provider and the customer, measured by the sustainability level of co-creation (Table 3.6), is strongly dependent on the mode of co-creation employed. In public transportation, where the customer exploits the service and passively co-creates value by creating the perception of value, the co-creation type is consumption or co-usage. By contrast, the co-creation type for the carpool is co-perform or co-production, as the customers share some of the tasks required to deliver the service and have to actively participate in trip coordination. Thus, in general, the sustainability level of co-creation in public transportation can be calculated based on the emissions of each passenger divided by the total emissions of the journey, which is represented by the quotient of one passenger to the total number of passengers. Hence, the more customers who co-create the service value (i.e., who use the service), the lower the relative emissions per customer. In addition, note that the sensitivity of the measure of total journey emissions to each customer co-creation process increases with the decrease in the potential total number of passengers. Thus, considering that a light rail trip in San Francisco may answer the transportation needs of 300 to 1000 passengers (60 passenger seats or 200 passengers total per railcar with five railcars per trip) (Cabanatuan 2010) while a bus can transport up to 70 passengers (50 sitting and 20 standing) and cars are typically limited to four passengers, the sustainability level of co-creation of the representative transportation services increases in the order of light train < urban bus < carpool.

CHAPTER 4

Physical Resource Assessment

At the heart of sustainability practice is the rational use of resources. Conceptualized in the term R^4, the rational use of resources begins with a *reduction* in the amounts of resources exploited followed by their *reuse* and *recycling*, and ending with their *recovery* or *regeneration*. In this sense, resources can be categorized as physical or nonphysical, e.g., material and energy or knowledge and methods, respectively. Moreover, systems for resource management have been developed based on a variety of environmental, social, and economic dimensions.

Nature exhibits the optimal use of physical resources as reflected in its efficient performance of multiple processes in concert. Most fundamental natural processes are performed in cycles that comprise the transformation of energy, elements (e.g., carbon or oxygen), molecules like water, and more complex matter such as nutrients in ecosystems. Likewise, many physiological systems, such as the cardiovascular and respiratory systems, also work in cyclical fashion, as do astronomical and climate cycles (e.g., day and night, and seasons of the years, which, in turn, determine agricultural cycles). Cyclical processes not only promote the sustainable use of physical resources and maximize efficiency, but also allow values to be transformed while controlling and regulating the process and performing various processes together. In addition, while ecosystem services are based on natural cycles, on the one hand, on the other hand, they also support nature's cycles. From the perspective of physical resource utilization, therefore, to reach the ultimate goal of sustainability, manmade processes should mimic the natural processes driving ecosystems, and in so doing, they should adopt and implement the rationale of cyclical processes.

Material Flow Analysis

The laws of mass and energy conservation constitute a fundamental component of physics and engineering. Likewise, the calculation of mass and energy balances is a basic tool used in the design and operation of processes. Insofar as they consider system inputs and outputs on the micro and macro levels, mass and energy balances can be used to calculate the economic, social, and environmental values of processes and products. In addition, the concept of resource flow analysis is also used to assess the sustainability of a variety of systems (Narayanaswamy et al., 2003), from goods and services to cities and countries, and is expressed many times in terms of the ecological or carbon footprint.

To demonstrate the practical meaning of sustainability of cities, the metabolism model (i.e., urban metabolism) was developed. In the frame of the metabolism model, city sustainability is assessed by measuring the total energy and materials that flow into the urban area (e.g., water, food, fuel, clothing, etc.) and emissions that flow out of it (e.g., air pollution, sewage, and solid waste) (Kennedy, Pincetl, and Bunje 2011). As stated before, for emissions, one of the most widely used measures is the carbon footprint. Calculated for cities, the carbon footprint can be used to compare between them, as in Table 4.1, where the carbon footprint was calculated based on electric energy and fuel consumption, tonnage and composition of landfill waste, and the amounts of steel, cement, and other materials or chemicals produced in the city and that cause non-energy related industrial process emissions.

Table 4.1 Greenhouse gas emissions for cities and metropolitan regions (Kennedy, Pincetl, and Bunje 2011).

City	Total emissions million t CO_2eq	Per capita emissions t CO_2eq
Bangkok	60.44	10.7
Barcelona	6.74	4.2
Cape Town	40.43	11.6
New York	85.87	10.5
Rio de Janeiro	12.11	2.1
Rotterdam	17.64	29.8

Life Cycle Analysis

Economic profit, always a driving force behind efforts to improve, stream-lines and changes product life cycles in terms of their associated goods and services and is usually also the incentive behind the development of new and alternative processes and products. Central to product life cycle improvements is the rational use of physical resources, which is also fun-damental to improving a product's sustainability and to conferring on the product life cycle previously lacking social and environmental values. Thus, the emergence of environmental awareness and the desire to develop pro-cesses that incorporate the rational use of resources and that have smaller impacts on the natural and social environments led to the introduction of the life cycle assessment or analysis (LCA) technique (Day 1981; Owens 1997; Finnveden et al., 2009). The LCA monitors the change in a value over the course of its life cycle, evaluates the impacts of resource utilization and discharge at all stages of the product life cycle, from "cradle-to-grave" (i.e., from creation to disposal), or from the perspective of a biomimicry approach, from "cradle-to-cradle" (i.e., waste-free life cycle).

Motivated by the economic struggles at the time, the LCA was first introduced in the 1970s, but it attracted renewed interest at the begin-ning of the 21st century with people's increased awareness of the need for environmental protection. In general, the LCA assesses the input and output of material and energy resources required for the whole pro-cess and the environmental emissions associated with the various activi-ties over the entire cycle. It is based on four main steps: (1) definition and scope—information needs, data specificity, collection methods, and data presentation; (2) inventory—process diagrams, data collection, and evaluation of the data, (3) impact assessment—determination of the im-pacts of each resource and their relative weights; and (4) improvement analysis—includes data evaluation and interpretation, conclusions and recommendations. Finally, in terms of the production and delivery of each resource, the output of LCA can be a list of the resources used or a single numerical value, like the carbon footprint, based on the integration of the total direct and indirect energies used.

The physical resource-based life cycle of goods is initiated by the ex-traction and processing of the raw materials and energy that are used in the second stage of the life cycle, manufacturing (Figure 4.1). The third stage of delivery, which includes actions such as packaging, storage, transportation, and marketing, leads to the fourth stage in which goods are used and, ideally, should be maintained. Finally, in the last, "end-of-life" stage of the life cycle, some of the resources are either returned to the cycle by reusing or recycling them in a closed format, or they are disposed of and thus exit the cycle.

Each step of the physical resource-based life cycle involves the utilization of various resources. In general, those resources can be categorized as direct resources added to the cycle during the process and indirect resources that were employed in the process environment, for example, those needed to run the facilities. In addition, some of the resources are incorporated in the final product while others are discharged from the process. Clearly, the two general types of resources have varied impacts on the economic-value of the cycle (e.g., the price of the good, the gross domestic product, etc.), but they also affect the ability of natural cycles to regenerate resources and to provide ecosystem services. Likewise, the resources consumed during the process that were not implemented in the final product but were emitted to the surroundings in the form of air emissions, sewage or solid waste, also affect the environment. This latter group of materials actually constitute pollution (i.e., foreign,

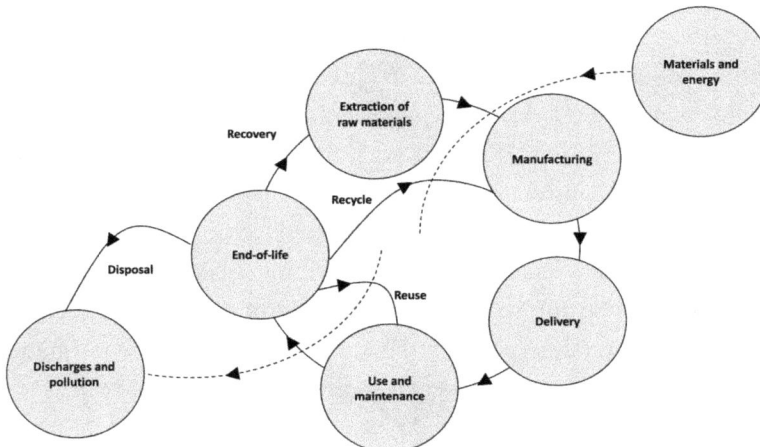

Figure 4.1 Physical resources-based life cycle

unwanted, and harmful substances released into the environment), and they have a marked impact on the environmental-value of the cycle. Finally, all stages of the goods life cycle also have social-values, from employment and working conditions, including fairness and equity, to labor laws and regulations to business ethics and the preservation of human rights.

As discussed earlier, one of the main routes to incorporate greater sustainability in any goods life cycle is through the use of CleanTechs or clean technologies. Defined as technologies that improve operational performance and process efficiency, CleanTechs are designed to reduce, with respect to a conventional goods or services, both the consumption of materials and energy, and the discharge of pollution to the surroundings (Pernick and Wilder 2007). Alternatively, reductions in natural physical resource use and the elimination or reduction of emissions and waste can also be achieved by adding a supporting and complementary service, i.e., CleanServs, to each stage of the life cycle (Wolfson, Tavor, and Mark 2013a, 2014; Wolfson et al., 2015). In addition, services are often coupled with goods in product-service systems. This yields more efficient solutions in the form of eco-efficient services and also reduces physical resource use and the discharge of pollution (Tukker 2004). Note that although service is, by definition, an intangible value or, in other words, a nonphysical resource, the service production and delivery process almost always involves the utilization of physical resources. For example, the provision of medical service by a doctor to a patient relies on the medical equipment needed for the examination and a computer on which the doctor can view the patient's medical history, document his or her diagnosis, and produce a prescription.

Circular Economy

From an economic point of view, the first phase of raw material extraction is mainly attributed to the primary sector of the economy, while manufacturing is a part of the secondary sector, and delivery is situated in the tertiary sector (i.e., services). The last two stages of the resources-based life cycle—use and maintenance and end-of-life —are usually a mixture of two but sometimes all three economic sectors. For example, recycling comprises the combination of garbage collection and separation services with the manufacture of recycled goods. However, the traditional linear economic model based on the three steps of "take, make, and dispose" is not concerned with creating or maintaining a closed cycle. As a result, processes based on this outdated model not only fail to reap the full potential or value of the process, but also harm natural cycles while depleting the pool of nature resources. In recent years, the general increase in awareness about sustainability and environmental quality, and the acknowledgement of the need for a novel approach to resources laid the seed for the idea of the circular economy (Ning 2001; Andersen 2007). This paradigm offers a restorative model according to which renewable resources are exploited to reduce the environmental impacts of goods. In addition, it suggests that every economic activity be designed such that the protection of nature and ecosystems is among its principal goals. Finally, it has strategic and operational benefits at both the micro- and the macro-levels.

Physical Resource-Based Assessment of a Service

Though today, either to maintain our lives or as a luxury, we use many more goods than we need, the main driving force behind the production of goods comprises our desires rather than our needs. The prevention or reduction of goods manufacturing is without a doubt the cheapest and most environmentally friendly approach. Nonetheless, for goods that are eventually produced, life cycle assessment could facilitate streamlining of the process and efforts to make them more sustainable.

Each stage of a good's life cycle comprises various steps and activities that differ from one good to another (Figure 4.1). For example, the detailed life cycle of a recycled paper bag, illustrated in Figure 4.2, includes: pre-manufacture—extraction of feedstocks (material and energy) and their transportation; production—from pulp and paper milling to the conversion of paper into bags; delivery—packaging and distribution to shops; and end use by the consumer, who chooses to either dispose of the bag as waste or to recycle it.

Boustead Consulting & Associates Ltd. performed a cradle-to-grave LCA of three types of grocery bags to inform the debate on the environmental

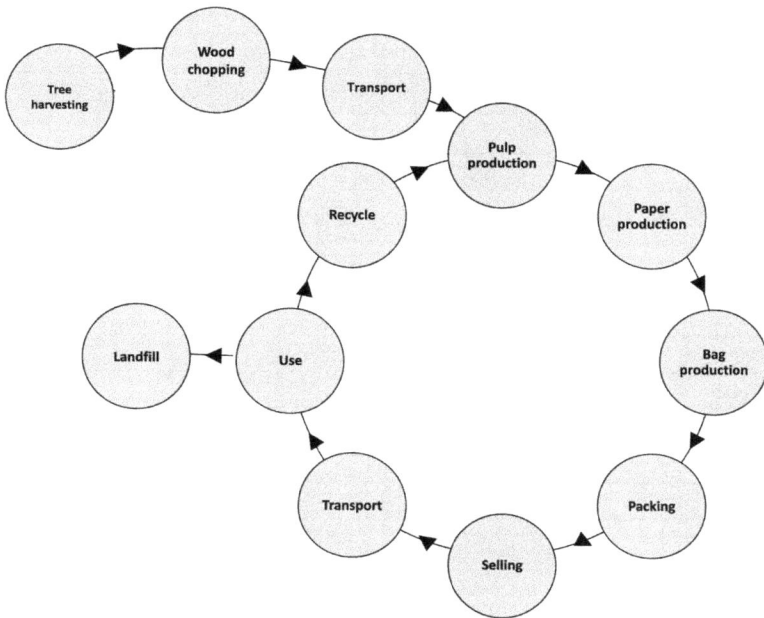

Figure 4.2 Life cycle of a recyclable paper bag

impacts of grocery bags and identify the types and magnitudes of environmental impacts associated with each type of bag (Chaffee and Yaros 2000). The resources (e.g., raw materials and energy) that were used and the wastes (e.g., air emissions, water effluents, and solid waste) generated over the course of the life cycle of 1000 paper bags of the type 1/6 BBL (30 percent recycled fiber) were assessed and quantified (Table 4.2).

With the exception of the use stage, all other stages in the life cycle of a paper bag, from tree harvesting and pulp milling to bag production and transportation, entailed energy use. Most of the fuels listed in Table 4.1 were consumed in the production of electricity, the main energy form that was used during the cycle, while fuel was also used for transportation. From among the total amount of energy consumed in the process, therefore, a very small part of it (e.g., the energy used to harvest the wood and produce the bag) was actually incorporated in the final product, while the rest, such as the fuel burned during transportation of the final product, has nothing to do with the production of the bag itself. Water, on the other hand, was used almost exclusively in

Table 4.2   Resources consumed and waste generated in the production of a recyclable paper bag

Resource	Amount	Resource	Amount
Energy (MJ)		**Air emissions (g)**	
Wood	1,521	CO_2	5,507
Oil	207	Methane	286
Gas	391	CO	121
Nuclear	127	SO_X	579
Biomass	24	NO_X	264
Other	352	Hydrocarbons	286
Total	**2,622**	H_2S	2.8
Raw materials (g)		HCl	7.1
Air	4,080	Dust	128
Clay	46.3	Other	34.8
Iron (Fe)	64.8	**Total**	**7,216**
Limestone ($CaCO_3$)	385	**Solid waste (g)**	
Phosphate as P_2O_5	147	Mineral waste	230
Sand (SiO_2)	101.6	Regulated chemicals	67.6
Sodium chloride (NaCl)	712	Waste to compost	1,290
Water	3,913,000	Wood waste	306
Other	344.8	Waste returned to mine	2,203
Total	**3,971,815**	Slugs/ash	947
Wastewater emissions (g)		Waste to recycle	2,544
COD, chemical oxygen demand	396	Other	393
BOD, biological oxygen demand	75	Recycled solid waste	-385
Chloride (Cl^-)	10.4	**Total**	**7,596**
Suspended solids	226.5		
Other (Metals, acids, dissolved solids)	252		
Total	**959.9**		

peripheral processes, such as cooling and the dissolution of other materials, after which it was discharged as an effluent. In addition, other compounds that were introduced into the process were emitted to the surroundings, either to the air, or as wastewater or solid waste. Furthermore, different emissions, like carbon monoxide and carbon dioxide, or nitrous and sulfur oxides, were formed during the process in the combustion of fuels. Finally, different types of solid waste were also generated by and transferred out of the process (Table 4.1), but the total amount of solid waste was reduced by the inclusion of some recycled bags during the production stage.

Addition of CleanServs

As previously stated, the addition of supporting and complementary services to the various stages of the life cycle can increase the sustainability of goods. More sustainable solutions can be realized by using the framework of clean services or CleanServs (i.e., services that are competitive with) if not superior to, their conventional tangible or intangible counterparts, that reduce the use of natural resources, and that cut or eliminate emissions and wastes while increasing the responsibilities of both provider and customer. Five types of CleanServs were offered, and in descending order from most to least sustainable, they are prevention, reduction, replacement, efficiency, and offset.

CleanServs can support reductions in the amounts of resources used and pollution emitted across the stages of a good's life cycle. The first type of services that were added to the life cycle of a good to improve its environmental impact is environmental services, or efficiency type CleanServs. Insofar as they are dedicated to the prevention or reduction of pollution after the use stage of a good, CleanServs are employed to close a good's life cycle by designing it to include the reuse, recycling, or recovery of resources as preferable alternatives to their disposal. Applied to the example of recyclable paper bags, CleanServs comprising the treatment and purification of the wastewater associated with the bag's life cycle (Table 4.1) can reduce not only the emission of contaminated water to the surroundings to prevent land and water pollution, but also the water footprint of the process by reusing the treated water in the bag production process.

Efficiency type CleanServs can also be added to the extraction and manufacturing stages and to the use and maintenance phases of a good's life cycle. Initial decisions about which opportunities offer the greatest potential to streamline the life cycle are typically made based on consultations and environmental surveys and assessments. The exploitation of research services that evaluate process improvement and redesign opportunities, market changes, and customer readiness to cooperate with prospective changes in a good's life cycle and to adapt their behavior to environmental changes can also augment the sustainability of the life cycle. Returning to the recyclable paper bag example, research can identify technologies that can be incorporated in the life cycle to decrease its associated discharges and can evaluate more fundamental changes to the process, such as the effect of using larger numbers of recycled bags in the production process. Additional services with the potential to increase the sustainability of the bag's life cycle include water and carbon footprint labeling on the bag and advertising the positive impact on the environment of choosing to use recyclable bags.

Taking a broader, more general perspective, there are also other types of CleanServs besides efficiency type that can be useful. For instance, by using information technologies like the Internet, services can eliminate redundancies in a good's life cycle to reduce physical resource use and emissions to the environment (i.e., reduction or replacement type CleanServs). In the traditional retail music industry, for example, the life cycle of the music CD comprises the following steps: recording the music, the production, packaging, and warehouse storage of the CD, delivery of the CD to a retail store, self-delivery of the CD from the store to the house, and CD use and disposal. But the number of CDs ultimately produced can be significantly reduced by using a reduction type CleanServ such as a CD rental or sharing service that encourages the use of the same CD by many people. Alternatively, music can be digitally downloaded (i.e., replacement type CleanServs) in the framework of a markedly different life cycle whose steps include recording the music and its storage on a database server from where it can be downloaded for private use. Although the two life cycles ultimately supply the same solution, a simple comparison shows that the digital option eliminates several important steps, such as the production, packaging, transportation, and disposal of the CD, in the process reducing the energy use and pollution emissions associated with the traditional retail music industry (Weber, Koomey, and Matthews 2009). Moreover, storage of the music in its digital form on a server instead of as a CD in a warehouse also reduces energy use. Indeed, for the entire life cycle, energy use is reduced from 53 MJ for the retail scenario to 7 MJ for the digital scenario (i.e., 87 percent reduction).

Physical Resources Assessment of a Service

Recalling that the provision of services also requires physical resources and goods, each service should also strive to be efficient in terms of its utilization of physical resources and the prevention or reduction of pollution emissions. To reach this goal, the physical resources-based life cycle of each service should also be assessed and improved such that the same flow scheme of goods (Figure 4.1) can be achieved, but via greener or more environmentally friendly services. However, in contrast to the myriad evaluations aimed at goods life cycles, relatively few reports have been prepared on services life cycles.

The physical resources-based life cycle of a Google search (Figure 4.3), for example, starts with a query that is entered by the customer and sent to the web server of the provider. That query is then transferred first to the index server, which matches the search terms to the pages that contain them, and then to the document server from which the stored document is retrieved. Finally, the search results are returned to the customer. An analysis of the Google search life cycle (Figure 4.3) shows that the majority of the energy consumed in the process—and thus, of the greenhouse gases emitted—is attributed to the energy required to run the customer's computer and screen. A quantification of the energy used by the customer, however, is not straightforward because it depends not only on the type and efficiency of the electronic equipment used by the customer, but also on the types of fuels used to generate the electricity consumed by the customer. Although these unknowns preclude a precise numerical assessment of the energy use involved in a Google search, it is estimated to be from 3 to 6 g CO_2eq per search. The carbon footprint of all the other steps is attributed to the provider (i.e., Google); dependent mainly on the energy source of the Google server farm, it is estimated at 0.2 to 0.5 g CO_2eq for each search.

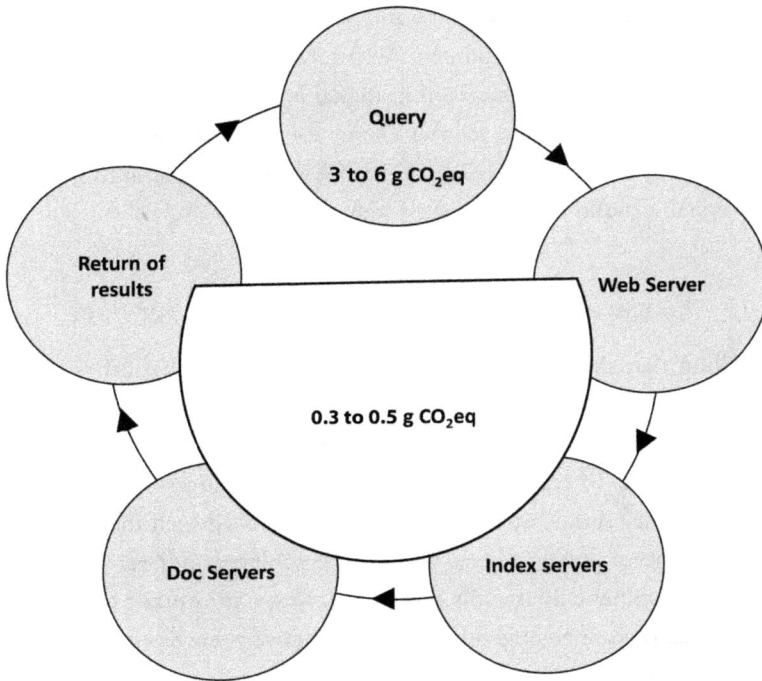

Figure 4.3 Carbon footprint of the Google search life cycle (Leake and Woods 2009; Google green)

The performance of a service life cycle assessment, a tool to increase the awareness of both customer and provider, can also be the basis for improving resource use throughout the entire life cycle. As such, a life cycle assessment provides indications of the potential changes that can be made in the different stages of the life cycle to effect more efficient resource use. For the Google search, for example, possible changes include the implementation of an energy saving project or the switch to greener energy sources at the provider's server farm. For their part, customers can use more electrically efficient equipment to increase the service's sustainability. More efficient energy use can also be achieved by improving the search efficiency of the Google servers and by encouraging customers to reduce the intensity of their search behavior by entering more precise and directed queries such that for each query fewer searches are needed (i.e., average energy use per query will fall).

Typically, a given good or service is not a stand-alone entity, as the life cycle of either a good or a service usually requires the input of different services or physical resources, respectively (e.g., delivery or distribution stage, Figure 4.1). For example, the life cycle of mail comprises the following steps: letter design, manufacturing of writing paper and envelope, production of the letter, distribution of the letter, use (i.e., reading) and disposal (Table 4.3). The distribution stage of letter mail entails various service steps as illustrated in the value chain in Figure 4.4 (Pitney Bowes Inc. 2008).

Numerous studies have dissected the life cycle of letter mail, breaking it down into its phases and evaluating each for its respective level of greenhouse gas emissions to determine the total amount of energy used (Table 4.3). Note that the distribution stage, which mainly comprises transportation and the running of physical facilities, accounts for the highest share of the emissions (around 70 percent).

The range of activities that constitute the value chain of the letter mail distribution service can be generally split between transportation-based steps and facility-based steps (Figure 4.4). Transportation resources refer to the fuel-related emissions associated with transport between facilities—from the initial mail collection point to the postal facility and from the postal facility to the customers—while facility resources comprise the emissions that are associated with the postal retail outlet, and the mail handling and sorting equipment. Each of the two activity groups is estimated to emit half of the total emissions linked to the distribution of a single piece of letter mail (i.e., 9 g CO_2eq per letter mail life cycle). However, these emissions can be markedly reduced by implementing CleanTechs and CleanServs, examples of which include, but are by no means limited to, using hybrid vehicles in the transportation of mail or powering postal outlet energy needs with solar energy and using a route planner service, respectively.

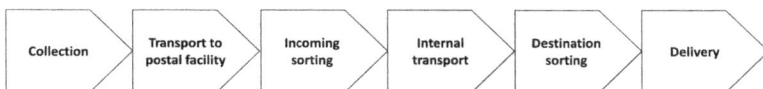

Figure 4.4 Value chain of a mail distribution service (Pitney Bowes Inc. 2008).

Table 4.3 Average greenhouse gas emissions of the life cycle of mail

Stage of life cycle	Main activities	CO_2eq (g)*
Letter design	Planning, data collection	0
Manufacturing of writing paper and envelope	Harvesting the wood, pulp and production	4.5
Production of the letter	Writing or printing	1.3
Distribution of the letter	Collection, transport, sorting, delivery	18
Use	Reading	0.05
Disposal	Landfill or recycling	~1
Total		~25

*Bases on one A4 paper that weight 4.5 g.

Finally, similar to the goods life cycle, service life cycles can also be improved by replacing them in part with digital alternatives, for example, online payment services can eliminate the need to drive to the bank or to the post office to pay bills, a move that can cut up to 99 percent of the emissions associated with the traditional bill payment services offered by the post office.

Outline for Sustaining the Physical Resources-based Life Cycle of a Service

To increase the sustainability of the physical resources-based life cycle of services, the following steps should be taken:

1. Describe the life cycle of the service with respect to resource use.
   a. Identify each step of the life cycle.
2. Assess the input and output of physical resources in each step.
   a. Data collection: direct and indirect resources, facility resources, discharges and pollution.
   b. Calculate relevant indicators and indexes.
   c. Identify steps with high resource use and pollution emission.

3. Search for CleanServs and/or CleanTechs that can prevent, reduce, or replace, or increase the efficiency of, each stage.

   a. Identify the steps in which the addition of CleanServs and/or CleanTechs holds the greatest potential for improvement.

   b. Search for relevant CleanServs and/or CleanTechs.

   c. Identify the constraints on and the limitations to implementing CleanServs and/or CleanTechs.

   d. Calculate the relevant indicators and indexes for comparing the alternatives.

CHAPTER 5

Sustainability as a Value

In general, each process can be presented as a series of actions and/or events that in combination produce a result or a product that can be either tangible or intangible (i.e., good or service). As such, every process can be schematically illustrated in linear form as a flowchart showing the step-by-step progression, in which a response to a step must be elicited before another step is taken. A nonlinear process, which is characterized by expansion in multiple directions rather than in a single direction, in contrast, is based on the concept that there are multiple starting points from where one can begin to approach a problem.

The manufacture of goods, as suggested by Porter's (1985) value chain, is typically a linear process that involves sequential steps characterized mainly by the flow and transformation of physical resources. In contrast, the value co-creation process of services is often nonlinear, and as such, the varying roles of the customer should be viewed as a constellation, as suggested by Normann and Ramirez (1993), accompanied by the flow and transformation of nonphysical resources.

Service Life Cycle

Nonphysical resources, which include information and knowledge, methods or tools, and time and effort, constitute the essence of the production and delivery of intangible values. But as discussed in previous chapters, service provision also involves the utilization of physical resources, and as such, the rational use of resources should be employed to increase the sustainability of services (i.e., green services). In addition, services can be exploited to increase the sustainability of the physical resources-based life cycle of goods (i.e., CleanServs). Likewise, the sustainability of a service must also be an integral part of service's core- and super-values (i.e., sustainable service).

The incorporation of sustainability initiatives in the nonphysical resources of a service environment is significantly more complex than doing so in a manufacturing environment. Unlike manufacturing, where the customer usually does not play an active role in the production process, in the service framework the customer is directly involved, to varying degrees, in the co-creation of value during the design, production, and delivery phases of the service (Vargo, Maglio, and Akaka 2008). In addition, in the manufacture of goods, we can identify two principal stakeholders with the capacity to actively affect sustainability: the first are the manufacturers that produce the products, and the second are the governments that implement rules and regulations, and that provide incentives to encourage sustainability in terms of both the end products themselves and the processes used to manufacture these products.

The two primary stakeholders in goods manufacturing are joined in the service provision process by a third stakeholder, the customer, who directly participates in the co-creation of the value. The fact that the customer is not a main stakeholder in the goods manufacturing process is not meant to imply that the customer has no input in the design of the manufacturing processes and products. Rather, in contrast to the case with services, customers are not directly involved in the value created by manufacturing processes. Thus, the co-creation process of a service must also be an integral part of the effort to increase the service's sustainability. From this perspective, customers in the scenario of service provision usually have not only more choice in the actions they can take to make the service more sustainable, they also have a greater responsibility to promote the sustainability of service solutions.

The nonphysical resources-based life cycle of a service, illustrated in Figure 5.1, is initiated by the planning and design stage, which comprises the identification of the value via a market survey as well as the organization of the various service components (e.g., people, tools, methods, infrastructure, resources etc.). The second stage entails the construction of the service value, so as to facilitate simultaneous production and delivery of the value in the next stage. Following delivery, the next stage is the use of the core-value, and the cycle is completed with the feedback and evaluation stage. In addition, to generate the core-value, different physical and nonphysical resources are introduced into the cycle in various stages,

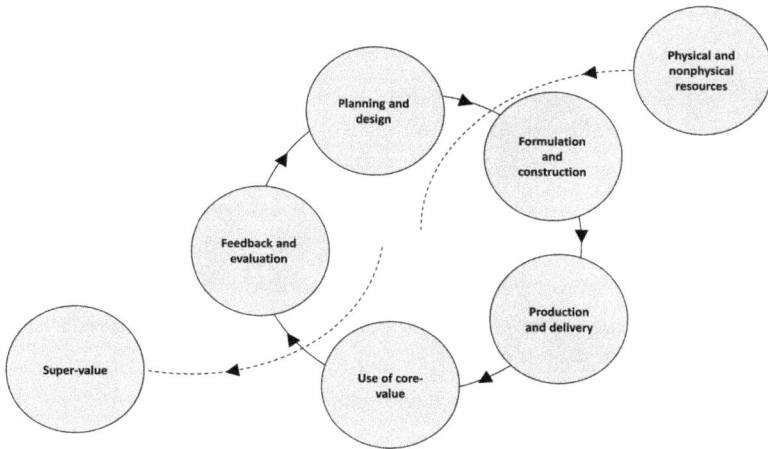

Figure 5.1 Nonphysical resources-based life cycle of a service

and other resources are released throughout the cycle. Yet the indirect effects of a service on the social and natural environments and the interactions of the service with other actors and processes constitute what is known as the service's super-value, a critical aspect of the service model that must also be considered in the nonphysical resources-based life cycle. At last, as previously mentioned, both the core- and the super-values of a service should be imbued with sustainability. Thus, assessments of the nonphysical-based life cycle of services can also promote increases in their levels of sustainability.

Sustainability and Added Value

In today's marketplace, many products, whether they are goods or services, are viewed as commodities. Thus, it is essential that sustainability be considered an added value that is integral to each good or service. In the framework of sustainability, added value refers to profits other than those yielded by the direct solution offered by a product (De Chernatony, Harris, and Dall'Olmo 2000). In terms of services, added value entails the provision of value that goes beyond the core-value (i.e., super-value). Hence, super-value is realized by introducing supplementary environmental, social, and economic values to the life cycle of a service.

One basic sustainability issue that should be discussed in terms of added value is the notion of the centrality of human beings and their supremacy and sovereignty over nature's biotic and abiotic elements. A multidimensional philosophical issue that is still a subject of spirited debate, it has evoked myriad theological, ethical, and political questions over the years. Broadly, world order vis-à-vis human beings can be conceptualized in three main ways: (1) anthropocentrism or human-centrism, in which human beings see themselves as the most significant species on the planet and as the center of the world, (2) biocentrism that views life as a main value, and as such, human beings are equal to all other species, and (3) ecocentrism that positions nature, including all of its biotic and abiotic components, as the central value. These conceptualizations raise fundamental questions about the "rights of nature", which refer to the rights of ecosystems to exist, flourish, and regenerate their vital cycles. Simple examples include nature's right to water, which ensures sufficient water flow in streams and rivers and the regular replenishment of underground aquifers, and the rights of animals to dignity.

User-centered, human-centered, and customer-focused designs have also become dominant themes in the design of goods and services. These people-first conceptualizations focus on the user's needs and abilities throughout the entire product life cycle to yield the most effective, efficient, and satisfying product. Yet, tailoring products to a particular target population usually renders them less suitable to other people. In addition, making customer needs the focus of product design, production, and delivery can negatively affect the natural environment, as it actually focuses on the wants rather than the needs of the user, and it presumably leads to an excess use of physical resources. At last, customizing a product to each customer also usually requires a larger investment of nonphysical resources in the process, and the resulting product is produced at a higher price than its generic equivalent. To increase the sustainability of a product, therefore, its design perspectives should also be altered from a human-centered to a life-centered approach that is supported with new sets of morals and ethics (Nash 1989). Moreover, as the existing legal framework and the dominant economic models view nature as human owned property and fail to protect it, realization of the added value of sustainability will require first the adoption of a new jurisprudence and economic paradigms that

recognize the inherent right of nature to exist, persist, evolve and regenerate, and that promote balance between human activities and the finite
natural resources of Earth.

Environmental Value

The rational use of resources and pollution prevention or control, which
are directly associated with the physical resources-based life cycle of goods
and services, constitute without a doubt one of the main dimensions of
environmental protection. As previously mentioned, they also indirectly
affect the ability of nature to maintain ecosystems and biodiversity (i.e.,
to sustain life). Yet the environmental value of a product is not determined solely in terms of a balance of physical resources.

The development of the new field of environmental ethics has played
an important role in laying the groundwork for the revision of outdated
environmental policies (Jeffery 2005). As ethics, or moral philosophy, are
in general based on the concept of right and wrong conduct, environmental ethics relates to responsible personal conduct with respect to natural
resources and nonhuman organisms and should therefore constitute a
fundamental part of sustainable development. Moreover, environmental
ethics also takes into consideration the moral obligations of human beings concerning the environment. Indeed, the steadily growing influence
of human activities on the Earth's ecosystems, driven by the increasing
human population, economic growth, and advances in technology (Kwak
and Freeman 2010), has stimulated wide ranging efforts to reframe environmental policies. To adopt an environmentally ethical approach and
preserve the "rights of nature", therefore, different concepts like "ecosystem health" (Costanza, Norton, and Haskell 1992) and "ecological
integrity" (Pimentel, Westra, and Noss 2000) were developed to assess
and measure the response of natural ecosystems to the stresses related to
human activity.

Similar to the scenario with human health, which focuses primarily on illness, for ecosystems, we usually measure ecosystem degradation,
such as contamination or loss of species, to determine the sustainability
of a value, instead of ecosystem health, which is defined as the capacity of the ecosystem to maintain biological and social organization while

achieving sustainable human goals. In general, three main ecosystem health properties can be described: (1) vigor or productivity—the capacity of the system to sustain the growth and reproduction of biodiversity, (2) organization—the capacity of the system to support the diversity of biota and their interactions, and (3) resilience—the capacity of the system to recover from disturbances. Likewise, ecological integrity can be defined as "the capability of supporting and maintaining a balanced, integrated, adaptive community of organisms having a species composition, diversity, and functional organization comparable to that of the natural habitat of the region" (Karr and Dudley 1981).

A variety of methods have been developed over the years to assess the health of ecosystems (Lu et al., 2015). These methods link human activity, regional and global environmental change, and reductions in ecological services with the consequences for human health, economic opportunity, and human communities (Wilkins 1999). The assessment begins by gathering physical and biological data: (1) biological indicators—biodiversity, biomass level, natality and mortality, and species growth rate, etc.; (2) physicochemical indicators—degree of air, water and soil pollution, and physical and chemical compositions, etc.; and (3) socioeconomic or human activity indicators—potential risks to human health, conservation of water and soil, and land use, etc. In the second step of the assessment, various indices that describe physical and biotic conditions are calculated and compared, in the third step, to a reference or historical date, which enables one to make informed decisions and to engage in effective ecosystem management.

The concepts of ecosystem health and ecological integrity are usually employed to assess the condition of an ecosystem, but they are also applicable to assessments of the environmental values of different services. In this case, however, instead of assessing the negative effects and the harm that the provision of a service can have on the environment, the benefits to the natural environment of the service are assessed. Clearly, every type of CleanServ that regulates physical resource use and pollution discharge has a positive impact on the environment, but there are additional, intangible environmental values, such as change of mindset or habits, that CleanServs can supply via their assigned core-values or that can be added to the CleanServ as a super-value. For example, insofar as it focuses on how natural environments function and how human beings can affect the sustainability of ecosystems for better or for worse, environmental education is a core-value that can be provided to change customer attitudes and that can intensify the mutual relations between people and nature. Another example is the addition to goods and services of sustainability labeling (e.g., carbon labeling, eco-friendly or 100 percent organic [Figure 5.2]) that allows customers to imbue their decision making processes with sustainability, thereby increasing the sustainability of the process (Cohen and Vandenbergh 2012).

During the last year, surveys taken about the influence of environmental impact labeling on product packaging on the consumption habits of customers indicated that environmental labeling indeed increases the awareness and the behavior of customers vis-à-vis eco-consumption (Guenther, Saunders, and Tait 2012; Grunert, Hieke, and Wills 2014). For instance, an assessment of the effect of applying carbon labeling to coffee packages on the purchasing behavior of Danish consumers indicated that the carbon label significantly influenced the purchase of coffee, although price and the Danish organic label were the most important determinants of product selection (Nielsen 2015). In another study, Vanclay et al., (2011) used sales data over the course of three months to examine the customer response to carbon labeling of groceries that were labeled using the "traffic light" theme: (1) green footprint—lower emission within each product range, (2) yellow footprint—average emission within each product range, and (3) black footprint—higher than average within each product range (Table 5.1). Their study compared the sales of 37 alternative brands distributed across the three product emission ranges from one month before until two months after the labeling was applied.

Figure 5.2 Eco-labeling

Table 5.1 *Effect of carbon labeling and price on grocery sales*

Labeling	Change of sales-labeling effect (%)	Change of sales-consistent labeling and price effect (%)	Change of sales-contradictory labeling and price effect (%)
Green	+8	+38	+33
Yellow	+13	+50	−24
Black	−19	−73	−13

In addition, they also evaluated the effect of the combination of carbon labeling and product price on customer choice.

As can be seen in Table 5.1, the addition of carbon emissions labeling to the products included in the study changed overall customer consumption habits slightly, regardless of the prices of the products, such that sales of the green labeled products showed an increase of 8 percent and yellow labeled by 13 percent, while sales of black labeled items with higher than average emission declined by 19 percent. However, analyses of product emission labeling in combinations with its price showed that when both the labeling and the price were consistent and lower than average (i.e., green labeled (lowest emissions) products and the lowest price), sales increased by 38 percent. Likewise, sales of black labeled products sold at higher than average prices declined by 73 percent. On the other hand, sales of green labeled products with contradictory prices that were higher than average rose by 33 percent while sales of black labeled products with low prices decreased by only 13 percent. Thus, it seems that increasing the environmental value of a product by adding carbon labeling is not enough to change the habits of most consumers, while the combination of environmental value with economic incentive (i.e., lower price) generates a synergistic effect that makes a difference.

Another environmental concept that has attracted much attention during the last decade is resiliency. Generally defined, resiliency refers to the extent to which a value can be provided in the present without infringing on the capability to deliver the same value in the future. The notion of resiliency promotes resource renewability instead of the less sustainable, conventional goal of a reduction in resource use. In other words, instead of emphasizing reductions in energy consumption, the focus should be on how to sustainably supply the amounts of energy needed. Resiliency is also a critical component of successful business management, a realm in which experience shows that typically more than 50 percent of businesses that lack effective resiliency plans ultimately fail following a major disruption (Ager et al., 2015).

In the framework of service dominant logic, resiliency can be achieved mainly by adding services to business operations, and as such, both the core- and the super-values of services should also be imbued with resiliency. Examples of resiliency-based services include forestry, which helps preserve habitats that sustain broad ranges of plants and animals, and captive breeding, such as species preservation efforts in wild reserves in which the animals are bred for subsequent release into the wild. In addition, resiliency can also be incorporated as a super-value in each service, for instance, the implementation of a carbon trading service that, through the exchange of carbon emission credits between businesses, can reduce emissions.

Social Value

Another option for imparting added value to a service is by including in the service life cycle extra social elements (i.e., social-value). At its most basic, social-value refers to the positive changes that a service's stakeholders experience in their lives. Broken down further, it can be described in terms of a distinction between outputs and outcomes, the former of which relates to the direct values gained during the service life cycle while the latter accounts for the large-scale effects of the outputs across space and time. Thus, social-value refers to the wider, nonfinancial impacts of processes and products, including increased equality, improved well-being of individuals and communities, and increased social capital and environmental sustainability. In practice, social-value is implemented through the preservation of the basic rights of both provider and customer during the production, delivery, and use of a service. In addition to the service's direct stakeholders, however, its other stakeholders, those indirectly involved in the process (e.g., employees, suppliers, other customers, and even future generations), must also benefit from the social-value of the service. Such indiscriminate enjoyment of social-value implies that it must extend beyond the social justice of each individual to include and collectively benefit the entire community.

Many services—education, health, and well-being among them—are social services by definition, and thus, their principal aim is to provide social-value. Indeed, in terms of the conventional service framework, in which services necessarily involve direct connections between provider and customer, the life cycle of any given service usually incorporates more direct social features than are offered in typical goods life cycles. However, recent years have witnessed the development of new technologies that facilitate novel service opportunities, and these are fundamentally different from conventional services. Perhaps the most significant of the new technologies comprises information communication technologies, such as self-services and e-services, which reduce to a minimum the extent and the essence of the contact between provider and customer.

The notion of social-value applied to a process or a business is not new. At its core is the principle that besides their pursuit of economical profit, companies or corporations must also behave in a socially responsible manner. Although this principle is deeply rooted in human history, the notion that entities such as businesses should take responsibility for the consequences of their actions, regardless of what is prescribed by the law, was defined at the beginning of the 20th century, but only since the 1950s did the idea attract significant interest.

The economist John Maurice Clark (1916, 1939) published extensive works about the *social responsibility* of businesses, *social control*, and *social economics*. He claimed that besides serving their own interests, businesses should follow ethical practices and engage in fair dealing. Clark also maintained that to achieve the goal of social economics, social control must be implemented to ensure the general welfare of all. Later, Theodore Kreps (1940) introduced the concept of the *social audit*, which entails an evaluation of the varied effects that businesses have on society and dictates that businesses report on the measures they take to ensure that their actions are also driven by social responsibility, an idea that was further developed by Howard Bowen, who coined the term *corporate social responsibility* (CSR) (1953). Yet while social-value practice between the 1950s and the 1970s focused on the positive actions taken by businesses that benefited society, the 1980s saw the convergence of economic and social interests, and firms became more responsive to their stakeholders' needs (Moura-Leite and Padgett 2011).

Bowen's concept of CSR, which, in addition profit maximization, considered the idea of social welfare, eventually led to the notion that businesses must also consider and weigh the legal, ethical, moral, and social impacts and repercussions of each of their decisions and practices. In addition, environmental concerns have also been an integral part of CSR, and during the 1990s, the idea of CSR spread across the globe until, at the dawn of the 21st century, it began to be incorporated as a fundamental part of business and firm strategies. Case in point is the establishment of *responsible care*, a global environmental, health, and safety initiative of the chemical industry to drive continuous improvement in performance and to promote transparency (Prakash 2000). Thus today, besides employee welfare and human rights, CSR also includes responsibility toward the environment and community development, and its implementation is recognized as a viable means to increase economic profit.

Embodied in the concept of CSR is the commitment of companies to their stakeholders (e.g., employees, shareholders, customers, partners, government and nongovernment organizations) to conduct business in an economically, socially, and environmentally sustainable manner that is transparent and ethical. One of the most accepted CSR evaluation and reporting instruments is the *global reporting initiative* (GRI) that was established in 1997 in partnership with the United Nations' Environment Programme (UNEP). Widely used around the world, the GRI provides all companies and organizations with a comprehensive sustainability reporting framework. In the framework of the GRI, the core elements of CSR include stakeholders, ethics and integrity, and economic, environmental, and social performances.

Although it enjoys widespread acceptance, the validity of the GRI has been questioned in works such as those by Porter and Kramer (2006), who argued that CSR is a generic concept that is disconnected from company strategy. As a result, it overlooks the opportunities that companies have to identify the social consequences of their actions and to benefit society. Moreover, they argued that the main problem with a reliance on CSR is that most companies focus primarily on their short-term performances, which necessarily narrows their perspectives vis-à-vis their customers and the value creation process. Therefore, they offered a new framework to evaluate the relationship between business and society that strengthens the competitive context in which businesses operate by redefining the purpose of businesses as creating *shared-value* (Porter and Kramer 2011). A management strategy that focuses on creating economic-value while identifying and addressing the social-values with which it intersects, the concept of shared-value connects societal progress with the bottom line of economic profit.

While both the service exchange and value co-creation processes are influenced by social forces (Edvardsson, Tronvoll, and Gruber 2011), the active engagement in service provision and value co-creation can, in turn, effect social forces. And as is the case with intangible environmental-values, social-values can also be added to both the core- and super-values of a service. First and foremost, every service provider and customer should ensure that the social rights (e.g., equity and security) of every direct or indirect actor of the service, from its current employees to members of future generations, are respected and preserved. For instance, a service that is not equally available or accessible to every potential customer (e.g., public transportation that is inaccessible to disabled people) is unsustainable. In contrast, services can also consciously supply positive social impacts, such as educational services imbued with social morals or services dedicated to assisting the poor or the elderly.

Economic Value

Economy, which can be simply defined as a network of activities that involves the management, transformation, and exchange of resources or products between people, is the main factor, the dominant logic, and the catalyst of most human activities and processes nowadays. Nonetheless, though every product has a *price tag*, the exact *value tag* of a product and how the value tag can be measured are not clear.

Actually a combination of art and science, the pricing of a product quantifies a wide range of factors and has many different models and strategies. The price of a product must cover all expenses, from physical and nonphysical resources, to labor costs, to marketing and sales, and even business maintenance, such as the return of loans. But because the product usually does not operate in a vacuum or separate from other products, the pricing of a product must be based on a thorough familiarization with the market, particularly as that concerns potential competitors but also in terms of both the return on investment and the risks for shareholders. However, one of the most important considerations in pricing comprises the customer and his or her needs, wants, habits, social class, etc., as these factors distinguish between the cost and the worth of a product and between the product's exchange-value and its use-value. The profitability of a product, therefore, is linked to both the satisfaction and loyalty of the customers whose decisions of whether to buy the product again are driven by their initial experience with the product and its corresponding perceived worth and use-value. But because the inherently subjective notion of value means different things to different people and because the same product can provide a variety of solutions and is used differently among people, the same product may also be assigned different value tags. Not only a mixture of production cost, market value and customer perceptions, a product's value tag is also the price we are ready to pay when we compare the benefits of one product with those of other products that offer similar or parallel solutions when comparing their prices. The value tag, therefore, adds an emotional element and the dimension of experience to the decision process.

Finally, the value and price of a product are also affected by the different phases of the product life cycle (e.g., production, delivery, and use) insofar as these phases can have tremendous effects on natural and social environments. Although the influence of value production and delivery on the environment and society has attracted increasingly greater attention in recent years, when it also became a part of law and regulation, and was incorporated into standard business practices, environmental and societal effects cannot be easily quantified or given a price tag. Finally, besides the product's price tag, the extent to which the product supports green growth and the development of entrepreneurship and innovation are also part of its economic value.

The essence of the relationship between environmental and social values and the economy is the subject of ongoing, vigorous debate on the issue of whether economy is part of the environment or vice versa (Figure 5.3).

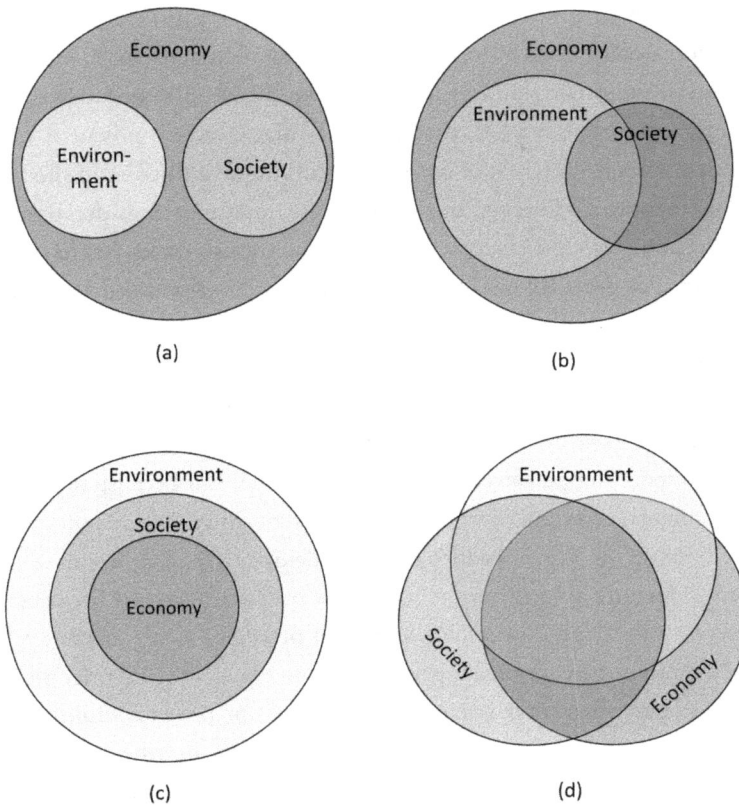

Figure 5.3 Relationships between economy, society, and environment in different economic models: (a) neo-classical economy, (b) environmental economy, (c) ecological economy, and (d) sustainable economy

Four general classifications of economy have emerged over the years. According to the *neo-classical economy* model (Figure 5.3a), economy is separate from nature. Nonetheless, because natural resources constitute a basic means of exchange, nature is perceived as a part of economy, but resource consumption is not a part of the model. The neo-classical model, however, recognizes the value of nature, which it interprets based on the willingness of people to pay for ecosystem services.

Environmental economy (Figure 5.3b), on the other hand, is an interdisciplinary model that considers both economic and environmental issues. It largely focuses on comprises market failures that occur as a result of markets failing to efficiently allocate resources, and on externalities, which refer to external effects that are not assimilated in the price tag, and on resources and products that are common or public. Thus, environmental economy offers tools, such as regulation, green tax, and pollution trade, to tie the economy with the environment.

The growing awareness of the urgency of environmental catastrophes such as climate change, and water and air pollution together with the acknowledgement that human actions influence the environment for better or for worse led to the creation of a new interdisciplinary philosophy and research field known as *ecological economy* or *eco-economy* (Figure 5.3c). Developed during the 1980s and 1990s, eco-economy deals with the mutual relations between human economy and ecological systems and is based on the idea that economic thinking and practice should be intertwined with and guided by physical reality, physical law, and biological systems. Although it recognizes the need of humankind to develop and achieve well-being, it also dictates that any development should be sustainable. As such, eco-economy distinguishes well-being from welfare, and it posits that the connection between economic growth and consumption is flawed. It argues that the assumption that consumption increases welfare is incorrect because welfare is not necessarily connected with well-being, and accepts that economic activity leads not only to positive, but also to negative effects on both the natural and the social environments. In addition, in contrast to neo-classical economy that sees natural resources as tradable means and environmental economy that perceives of environmental effects as indirect or outside influences that should also be priced, eco-economy implies that the economy is a subdomain of environment.

In identifying economy as subordinate to environment, eco-economy emphasizes the fundamental importance of natural capital and ecosystem services and the limited carrying capacity of the Earth. From that perspective, it aspires to develop theories and tools for the development of *sustainable economy*, which comprises economic systems that can exist for extended periods and sustain the society (Figure 5.3d). In practice, therefore, sustainable economy implies that a company must pay for the overall effects that their operations have on the world, and it also places a price on external company effects (Chouinard, Ellison, and Ridgeway 2011). In addition, it considers the *whole life cost* or *life cycle cost* of a process, from cradle-to-cradle or cradle-to-grave, which accounts for the direct and indirect economic, social, and environmental costs associated with an economic system.

The sustainability of a service can be incorporated into the pricing of a service by combining its exchange-value with its use-value. Sustainable pricing should also account for and integrate the effects of the service's provision on ecosystem services and on human health and quality of life. One way to include environmental-value in the sustainability of a service is through the implementation of an *environmental tax*, also known as *eco-tax* or *green tax*. Eco-taxes are government measures intended to encourage authorities, businesses, and people to adopt more environmentally friendly operational modes by levying a tax on products, practices, or activities that are considered harmful to the environment. However, the main goal of eco-taxes—to ameliorate or eliminate the negative impacts that processes have on the natural environment by affixing a monetary tag to pollution—risks perception of this tax as actually another external cost that, accordingly, producers will include in the final price of the product such that it is actually paid for by the customers. Alternatively, the harmful environmental impact of processes can also be reduced by subsidizing those authorities, businesses, and people that add environmental-value to their process, which entails the promotion of environmental policy through financial means. Some examples of eco-taxes or *environmental subsidies* that are also applicable to the service sector are listed in Table 5.2.

Table 5.2 Environmental taxes and subsidies

Tax/Subsidy	Explanation
Carbon tax	Carbon pricing of greenhouse gas emissions from the use of fuels
Renewable energy subsidy	Subsidy to encourage the use of renewable power
Electronic waste recycling fee	Tax imposed on new purchases of electronic products to encourage recycling
Public transport subsidy	Subsidy to provide and maintain quality public transport services
Landfill fee	Tax imposed on waste landfill to encourage recycling

Economic-value can also be sustainably added to the production and delivery of services by using the *local economy* and *green growth* models, which promise development and a widening of market opportunities in a way that does not harm the social or natural environment, but instead actually confers benefits on both. However, as globalization has transformed the world into a global village, the challenge of exploiting the local economy, which entails that one strives to "buy locally", has become more formidable than ever despite the clear benefits. A flourishing local economy is based on a wide variety of supporting services that must also be obtained locally, thereby leading to lower emissions and levels of pollution. In addition, money spent at the local level stays in the community, helping to sustain it and generating more local business in a cyclical process. Indeed, the struggle between local business and huge corporations has myriad effects on our lives, and the benefits range from fairer prices, to increased employment levels, to the conservation of nature's capital. Services are also an integral part in the development of the green growth paradigm, which refers to economic development built on steadily increasing output without adversely affecting either the environment or society. No longer a luxury, the adoption of approaches directed by the green growth paradigm should be seen as an imperative for sustainable development.

CHAPTER 6

Trends in Service Science

Sustainable strategies and practices are equally applicable to both service operations and manufacturing operations. In parallel with the increasing importance of the service sector, the process comprising the production and delivery of services has undergone tremendous change that has been driven by human needs, the ever-growing wealth of human knowledge, and the technological opportunities generated by that knowledge. The ultimate result entails specifically tailored solutions that increase end-user satisfaction, on the one hand, while improving the performance, efficiency, and productivity of the service, on the other. In addition, the production of services usually requires relatively less natural capital and more human capital than the production of agricultural or industrial goods. Service sector growth, therefore, puts less strain on the environment.

Value Co-creation

The rapid development and implementation of new technologies together with the emergence of service dominant logic has not only dramatically changed how we produce and deliver services, but it has also expanded the opportunities in the service sector. Traditionally, most services were provided in a person-to-person mode, in which the supplier and the end-user or consumer met face to face or communicated directly, for example, by telephone. Moreover, it usually followed the value in-exchange model where the supplier possessed most of the knowledge and invested the majority of the resources and facilities as well as the manpower to produce and deliver the value to a consumer who subsequently used that value. Today, however, most services are provided via the value in-use model, where values are jointly and reciprocally co-created by the provider and the customer through a range of different types of interactions between the two (e.g., e-service).

The value co-creation process requires that the physical and nonphysical resources (e.g., energy and materials, facilities, effort, and information and knowledge) be divided between the provider and the customer. The sustainable division of investments and tasks between the two, therefore, should consider not only the efficiency of the service's provision with respect to materials, energy, time, and effort, or the abilities and requirements of provider and customer, but also the needs and rights of all other stakeholders throughout the value chain. The variety of co-creation opportunities are many and varied, but they can be pursued in three general modes: (1) *self-service*—the provider provides a platform for use by the customer, who invests knowledge, skills, and facilities to execute most of the service (Figure 6.1a); (2) *mixed-service*—the provider and the customer share equally in the responsibility for most resources (Figure 6.1b); and (3) *super-service*—most resources and tasks are supplied by the provider (Figure 6.1c) (Campbell, Maglio, and Davis 2011; Wolfson, Tavor, and Mark 2012).

However, new insight into the role of the customer in the service provision process resulted in the development and expansion of the self-service mode, which today includes daily activities that exploit ubiquitous service opportunities, like pumping one's gasoline at a self-service filling station and withdrawing money from an ATM. Moreover, the exponential pace of information and communications technologies development, especially of the Internet and associated software applications, have tipped the scales in favor of digital self-services, or e-services, which are delivered over the Internet and whose security is ensured by dedicated information

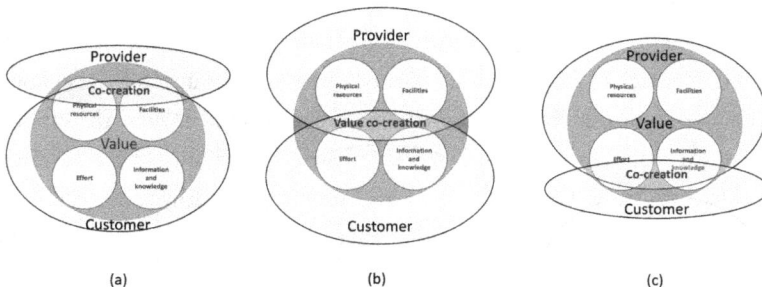

Figure 6.1 Various service modes: (a) self-service; (b) mixed-service; (c) super-service

technologies while requiring minimal human intervention. Common examples include e-booking of concert tickets, filling out and filing of governmental forms, and bill payment. Digital services, however, are not limited to e-services that supply intangible value. They also include e-commerce, which refers to a product-service system in which purchases are made on the Internet.

Consider, for instance, a bill payment service (Table 6.1). In a traditional, person-to-person mixed-service, the customer arrives at the bank or the post office to pay the bill via the clerk, a service that requires a relatively large number of resources, including facilities and manpower. Alternatively, customers can pay their bills by using a call center, which not only eliminates the need to go to the bank, but also requires much simpler office facilities and surrounding services, and as such, it reduces the resources used, both physical and nonphysical, by the service. In addition, the call center offers not only a more flexible, available, and accessible service to the customer, who can exploit the service without having to travel at any time of day and from almost any location, it usually also necessitates less effort from both the customer and the provider. An even more flexible and less time consuming alternative to the call center for bills payment is the e-service self-service mode, which is built on a more intense investment by the customer, who needs a computer or mobile device and knowledge, to be able to use the service. Furthermore, e-services transfer responsibility for most of the tasks and resources from the provider to

Table 6.1 Division of main resources and capabilities of a bill payment service

	'Person-to-person'		Self-service (e-service)	
	Provider	Customer	Provider	Customer
Materials and energy	Electricity, water, etc.	None	Electricity, water, etc. (less)	Electricity
Facilities	Office and equipment	Mode of transportation	Office and equipment (less)	Computer
Effort	Manpower and time	Arrival to office and time	Manpower and time (less)	Time
Information and knowledge	Clerical work	None	Clerical work (less)	Computer operation

the customer, and they usually consume fewer overall resources and are much more efficient than their conventional equivalents. However, because the use of e-services requires certain facilities and knowledge, they do not necessarily suit every customer, and they also raise several social issues such as equity and accessibility.

However, the self-service mode is not always the most sustainable choice for every service opportunity. To complete one's weekly grocery shopping, for example, instead of physically going to the supermarket to buy the groceries, a customer can use a grocery ordering super-service via the telephone or the Internet, thereby precluding his or her need to travel to the supermarket while allowing the provider to more efficiently manage its grocery delivery service. Although using this mode of service assigns most of the responsibilities for the associated resources and tasks to the provider, it relies essentially on co-creation by the customer who, for example, composes the shopping list. Moreover, this service mode may also lead to much more accurate and calculated shopping driven mainly by customer needs and unaffected by the many temptations to which customers are exposed when they shop in a self-mode (e.g., advertisement, campaigns, etc.). This is especially true in today's supermarkets, which typically have been carefully engineered to maximize customer spending through impulse buying.

As noted in Chapter 5, human-centric services constitute one of the recent trends in service provision. In general, insofar as they seek to increase both customer satisfaction and also the price tag of the service, human-centric services can potentially consume more physical and nonphysical resources than "generic services." Moreover, they are usually implemented to produce and deliver luxury services, which cater to the wants, and not the needs, of the customer. Therefore, inherent to human-centric services is a potential to discriminate based on social-values like equity and accessibility or availability. Nonetheless, as human-centered services target specific populations with more precisely defined requirements and whose abilities and ways of thinking are known, they also entail an opportunity to divide the tasks and resources more effectively between provider and customer and to perform the service more efficiently. As such, the design of sustainable human-centered services can also add new and specific values to the services. For example, the provision of health services to the elderly at their homes instead of at a clinic or a hospital not only provides each customer with the precise treatment they need, but also streamlines the service in terms of resource use, as it eliminates the need for the patient to reach the clinic, and with respect to the management of the schedule of the service providers (e.g., doctor, nurse, etc.). Furthermore, human-centric services can also be exploited by designing a service to include environmental and social benefits that are important to a target population of customers. This can include basing the production and delivery of a service solely on renewable energies, even if the ultimate monetary cost of the service to the customer is higher than that of a conventional equivalent.

The provision of self-services or human-centric services, which are more flexible and accessible as well as more specific and tailored to the wants of each customer, may also lead to a *rebound effect* (Berkhout, Muskens, and Velthuijsen 2000). Under the rebound effect, the more efficient provision of cheap products has the potential to lead to consumption overload, which describes increases in the purchase of a product or more extensive use of the same product. For example, reductions in the price of electricity can result in higher electricity usage per capita or offering an efficient plastic bottle recycling service can cause people to purchase more plastic beverage bottles. Likewise, although e-services can be simply and effectively used by customers from almost anywhere and at any time of the day, on the one hand, on the other hand, they can promote much more intensive use of services. Thus, the ease with which they can be used favors their unintentional abuse, a scenario in which the services are run even when they are not actually required, resulting in the more intensive use of resources. A common example of e-service overuse is searching the Internet using services such as Google. Used daily by millions of people on an hourly basis, often, the search is not defined clearly enough or even necessary.

Shareconomy

The ever-increasing pace of the acquisition of goods and services, also known as consumerism, is one of the most deeply rooted problems of modern society (Miles 1998). Consumption, the process by which values are purchased and used by people, in fact marks the end of a linear chain of economic activities that start with the extraction of resources, and then proceed to the production of goods and services to their eventual distribution among consumers or customers. The effect of the linear consumption process on the economy is enormous: it promotes manufacturing and commerce as well as employment, and it accelerates *economic growth* that, in turn, leads to growth in potential output. However, growth in this sense can take a heavy toll in terms of natural resource depletion, the generation of emissions, effluents, and waste, and the enhancement of worker exploitation and inequity.

The mass consumption or consumer society in which we live worships materialism, and perhaps accordingly, the dominant value-system measures people based on their assets. In the modern Western world, the majority of people use far more natural resources and live much less sustainably than in the rest of the world. In fact, most people in the West enjoy the benefits of increased productivity without considering its consequences. However, beside the fact that people definitely do not need most of the things they buy for their survival or to live a good life and flourish, they are usually used for only short proportions of their lifetimes if they are used at all. For example, the private car, which already long ago became a basic commodity rather than a luxury in the West, has many advantages for its owner, such as flexibility and accessibility, in the framework of the car's main value, on-demand 'door-to-door' travel. But the human reliance on the private car has a relatively high cost per average person-miles traveled compared to other modes of transportation, such as bus and train, and a much greater negative impact on the social and natural environments. That cost, studies have shown, is due in part to the fact that vehicles are used on average only 5 percent of the time and that they spend a substantial percentage of time parked rather than being driven. Indeed, according to the 1995 UITP Millennium Cities Database, data collected from 84 cities around the world showed that the cars in these cities were parked 95.8 percent of the time and in motion for an average of only 61 minutes a day. Likewise, the Royal Automobile Club Foundation in the UK reported in 2012 that the typical car in the UK is parked 96.5 percent of the time (Kenworthy and Laube, 2001; Vivier 2006). A lot can be learned from these statistics, which show that in addition to the exorbitant expenses associated with the production and ownership of private cars, the resources consumed in the car manufacturing process and by all relevant peripheral services (e.g., road construction, insurance, etc.) are actually not used efficiently. Unfortunately, this trend is not limited to automobile manufacturing, as the same disregard for and waste of the limited resources available on Earth are also associated with many other goods, e.g., televisions, clothing, etc. In similar fashion, however, many nonphysical resources, like time, knowledge, and skills and services, are also not always used efficiently and rationally.

The roots of the material culture can already be found in Europe in the early modern time, around the 17th century, and the culture continued to grow throughout the 18th century. However, the ability to mass produce many goods cheaply during the industrial revolution of the 19th century begat modern capitalism—the economic and political system in which trade and industry are controlled by private owners for their profit. It also accelerated the consumption of goods while yielding the consumer culture. The institutions associated with *mass market economy* transformed, mainly since the middle of the 20th century, the culture, ideals, and politics of Western society, and today, similar systems are also prevalent in the East. In recent years, however, recognition of the marked stress that this culture places on nature as well as its economic, social, and environmental costs has led to the revival of more traditional market concepts such as barter, cooperative use, and sharing of values.

The need to streamline resource utilization with respect to its economic and environmental costs while expanding market opportunities and sustaining a continuous process of technological advancement, particularly as that applies to the digital revolution, have led to the quest to generate new values and to do so using alternative methods. In addition to a focus on new ways of doing things, these efforts also stressed competiveness, resulting in the emergence of new economic models such as *collaborative consumption* or *collaborative economy* (Botsman and Rogers 2011; Leismann et al., 2013), *peer-to-peer economy* (Vishnumurthy, Chandrakumar, and Sirer 2003), *on-demand economy*, *access economy*, and *sharing economy* or *shareconomy* (Meade 1986; Heinrichs 2013). The basic motivation behind all of these models is the utilization of underexploited values by using a framework in which everyone can act as both provider and customer. In addition, recognizing the power of the individual, it also made redundant the need for brokerage. Despite the commonalities between these models, however, they differ on many counts and are often confused with one another.

The term collaborative consumption, which refers to the use of digital technology to reinvent and intensify traditional market behaviors such as renting, lending, and sharing, was coined by Felson and Spaeth in 1978 (Felson and Spaeth 1978). A collaborative consumption economy comprises a system driven by network technologies that match 'needs' and 'haves' of underused values by connecting directly between provider and customer without a mediator. Similarly, an on-demand economy is a system based on directly matching customer needs with providers to deliver goods and services immediately; a peer-to-peer economy refers to a model whereby two individuals interact directly with each other to buy or sell goods and services without intermediation by a third party; and an access economy is a model where values are traded on the basis of access instead of ownership, and a company functions as the mediator between provider and customer. Finally, a shareconomy is an economic system that connects individual stakeholders to facilitate their direct sharing of resources, assets, goods, and services. In such a system, ownership is replaced by access, and consumer behavior is not limited to merely searching for resources, assets, services, and goods to be acquired and owned. In addition, it allows individuals to profit more from their assets, knowledge, and skills. Shareconomy encourages the interaction of multiple providers and customers, and its participants can be providers one time and customers another time, or they can even play both roles simultaneously. It also allows the disaggregation of physical resources and assets, and their consumption as services, and insofar as it forms direct connections between people and fosters among them feelings of community, the shareconomy also has a strong social impact. Although today, the term shareconomy is widely and commonly used to encompass a wide range of barter, cooperative, and sharing structures, in many cases, this designation is incorrect.

Advances in technology have greatly facilitated collaborative and sharing activities, resulting in tremendous growth in all of the above-mentioned models in recent years. These new concepts have already penetrated many sectors, for example, accommodation and transportation, and in the process, they have transformed the way we consume and use values. Not limited to big businesses, the opportunities offered within these new frameworks are already regularly exploited by individuals on a large scale. Finally, in general, all the above-mentioned models incorporate services as a platform for collaborative or sharing activities.

Although the sharing of physical and nonphysical resources is not a novel concept, recent developments in the field have added a variety of sharing levels and models based on the recombination of conventional values in new ways. Thus, in contrast to a scenario in which people use their resources (i.e., car, computer, knowledge, etc.) when they work, sharing the same assets when they are not being used through different sharing mechanisms can be considered a shareconomy-based approach. Similarly, using product-service systems of the rent or lease types can also be included, to some extent, in the framework of shareconomy.

In general, there are four main categories of sharing: (1) recirculation of goods—repeatedly reusing goods, for example, from second hand shops or platforms like eBay, (2) increased utilization of durable assets—using assets to their full capacity, for example, renting a room via AirBnB, a car for a short time through Zipcar, or a ride with Uber, (3) exchange of services—for instance, TimeBanks that allow the trading of services based on time invested, and (4) sharing of productive assets—sharing place, real or virtual, to enable production instead of consumption, for example, a food cooperative or co-working hub.

Because the shareconomy is a socio-economic ecosystem that enables the sharing of both human and physical resources, the shareconomy categories have varied impacts on both the social and the natural environments. In addition, shareconomy alters the marketplace, transferring it from the street to the virtual space and also facilitates new market opportunities to which can be added sustainable values. First of all, insofar as the shareconomy platform presents an opportunity to cut the prices of goods and services by using unused products and avoiding the need for intermediaries, it offers economic benefits. Additionally, the creation of new markets that are based on the opportunity of every person to be both a provider and a customer not only expands the volume of commerce, it also confers more power on the individual and changes the relative share of small and local businesses in the economy.

The environmental benefits of sharing are clear, from reductions in the demand for new goods driven by the reuse of old goods and the development of secondary markets, which decrease the physical capital resources that are invested in new goods, to the more efficient use of resources during the use stages of the goods' life cycles (i.e., increasing the lifetimes and use intensities of goods). The new marketplace also reduces the need for large storage and exchange facilities for goods (e.g., shops, warehouse, etc.) and eliminates the need for the customer to be physically present in the shop to make a purchase or for the provider to engage in sales activities such as marketing and advertisements. Thus, exploiting the new marketplace enables reductions in the amounts of physical resources consumed during the delivery stage.

However, insofar as the shareconomy platform eases and promotes consumption, and offers goods and services that are identical to those offered in the conventional economy but at lower prices, it can also generate a rebound effect manifested as an increase in the numbers of unnecessary goods that are purchased. Indeed, a simple comparison of the resource use associated with one-on-one deliveries to those consumed through the mass delivery systems of big business shows that the former is usually markedly less efficient in terms of physical resource use, but that evaluation should also include the electricity that is used during the search and purchase of goods and the secondary services that are involved. In addition to rational use of physical resources, the shareconomy should also incorporate other environmental values, such as changing customer attitudes toward the reuse of goods and instilling greater environmental awareness in its participants.

Shareconomy also has many potential social impacts. First, in some cases it changes basic interactions between provider and customer, because it does not necessarily require direct communication between the two and can even allow both sides to remain anonymous. In contrast, for provisions that require high levels of interpersonal interaction, the social impact of the shareconomy increases. Another important social ramification of shareconomy concerns the equity of every customer and provider in terms of possessing the necessary devices and knowledge to use the new sharing platform. Implementation of a shareconomy approach will also exact significant changes in the workplace and the worker market. Initially, though some traditional jobs will become scarcer, the shareconomy will offer entirely new job opportunities. For instance, people will be able to use their private cars as taxicabs to work part time as taxi drivers. There is also lively debate about unpaid labor from crowds of volunteers as, for instance, people who write entries in Wikipedia. Finally, a shareconomy also raises numerous legal issues, as many of the currently used sharing systems evade regulations and even break the law. In addition, there are also security issues, from income guarantees, to the financial risks to providers, to the physical security of both the provider and the customer. Moreover, while large firms and companies are obliged to operate with some extent of transparency, the activities that occur via shareconomy platforms are usually not transparent.

Thus, to fulfill the new ideas of coupling economic, social, and environmental values by doing good, building new social connections, saving the natural and social environments, and providing new opportunities and benefits to all people, there is a need to sustainably define and modify the structures of the shareconomy.

Some claim that there is no real difference between capitalism and the first two categories of the shareconomy (i.e., recirculation of goods and increased utilization of durable assets), as these types of shareconomy merely involve different exchange mechanisms. Additionally, though these two share categories are today the most widely used and recognized shareconomy activities, they are defined more by consumption, rather than production, of values. Furthermore, while the production and delivery of values in the frame of these two categories require some measure of co-creation, the value transfer mode is closer to value in-exchange rather than to value in-use, as the consumer pays for a product, either a good or a service, which he or she receives from the supplier. In addition, while under the goods reuse category, the customer still owns the good, the second category—that of increased utilization of durable assets—is based on assets owned by the provider and rented to the customer. These two categories are actually based on product-service systems, and therefore, they are not really sharing models but servicizing models that resemble reuse mechanisms such as flea markets, give and take markets, and traditional rental services.

Therefore, to make these new exchange platforms more sustainable, extra values (e.g., as were discussed in Chapter 5) should be added to the product-service systems. Such extra values can include anything from ensuring the security of the provider and/or of the customer and allowing everyone to participate in the process (i.e., social-values) to the transport of multiple items in the same shipment (i.e., environmental-value). In addition, because the notion of shareconomy is to co-produce something for mutual benefit, it is essential that *shared-values* be added to the process. For example, instead of simply renting a car from a company like Zipcar or using the Uber platform to rent a ride, each of which is a product-service system, the use of carpooling, which allows any owner of a private car to share that car with other passengers and to be either a passenger or a driver, is actually a sharing activity in which value is co-produced and not just consumed.

The two other categories of sharing, service exchange and the sharing of productive assets, are based mainly on intangible values and their co-creation. As such, they are driven by the nonmonetary exchange of nonphysical resources, and as a result, they also usually involve greater social interaction. Yet service exchange in the frame of shareconomy is not just about service provision or the bartering of one service for another, it should also create new values, which are actually shared by the provider and the customer, beyond the core-value. The challenge, therefore, is to create a resource pool that can be used together and not only exchanged, from platforms like Wikipedia that foster the sharing of knowledge and information to file sharing services that facilitate user access to shared documents to Facebook and other online social networks that allow myriad intangible values to be shared. But from among the existing categories of sharing that of the sharing of productive assets possesses the highest sharing level. A common example includes the cooperative use of tangible or intangible values that are owned, managed, and operated by a group of people (i.e., a cooperative), from grocery stores to information or experience sharing platforms.

Examples

It is usually assumed for long-lived electric equipment that an increase in the number of uses can significantly decrease the energy embedded in the material extraction and production stages of the life cycle compared to the energy consumed in the use stage (Downes, Thomas, and Walker 2011). For example, a life cycle assessment of a laundry machine, an electrical appliance that can be found in most households, showed that the energy used to extract the raw materials (e.g., iron, steel, and plastic) and during the production phase of the machine corresponds to 15 to 25 percent of the total energy of the cycle, depending on the brand and size of the machine (Garcia 2013). If the average lifetime of a laundry machine is 10 years, and the machine is used on average for one hour every two days, then each machine is used 180 times a year. In this scenario, the machine is actually in use less than 2 percent of the time, while 98 percent of the time it is idle. Although the resources used for each load of laundry (e.g., electricity, water, and detergent) are more or less equal, the more the machine is used, the lower its emissions (corresponding to machine production) will be per load. This simple analysis shows that the physical resources invested in the life cycle of the washing machine in terms of its production are not managed efficiently. Therefore, the contributions of the equivalent greenhouse gas emissions and water used in the equipment life cycle to the carbon and water footprints of each load are high.

A viable alternative to the ownership of a personal laundry machine is the use of a product-service system offered by a Laundromat, where the typical washing machine is in use for 10 hours each day, and thus, the carbon and water footprints of each load are significantly cut. Stated simply, if the average carbon footprint of a load of domestic laundry is 700 g CO_2eq and 20 percent of the emissions (140 g CO_2eq) correspond to the production of the machine, then doing one's laundry in a typical Laundromat will cut the emissions attributed to the machine production phase by 90 percent per load and reduce the carbon footprint of each load to 574 g CO_2eq. Moreover, as the machines in a Laundromat are usually more efficient in terms of energy and water use per kilogram of laundry and because the Laundromat buys its equipment, detergents, and other supplies in large volumes (i.e., less emission during delivery), the emissions attributed to the use of the machine become lower still (Hu et al., 2012). Furthermore, the Laundromat can be equipped with a suitable water recycling system, which would cut both the water use of the system (i.e., water footprint) and the amounts of effluents tremendously.

To cross the gap from a product-service system in the form of a Laundromat to a shared service, a domestic laundry machine can also be shared by smaller groups, whether they comprise extended family members, friends, or neighbors (i.e., increased utilization of durable assets). Yet this type of shared assets also requires coordination. Furthermore, it should be considered that while the resources invested in each load of laundry (i.e., core-value) are the same, the resources behind the creation of the super-value and associated with driving to the home where the machine is located are different. In another scenario, a domestic laundry machine can be purchased in a cooperative model by a group of people, such as neighbors or the employees in an office, such that each member of the group shares in the ownership of the machine, which is used and operated by all the group's members. In addition to its higher sharing level, the cooperative model also entails different social-values, for example, everyone has the opportunity to be a part of the cooperative. Finally, the platform can be supplied with extra values, such as instructions about how to efficiently use the machine, the ideal temperatures at which the laundry should be washed, and even the recommended number of times per year specific types of clothing should be washed.

CHAPTER 7

From Single Service to Whole Service

The transfer of a service from provider to customer via a value co-creation process comprises a set of activities that can be performed in series or in parallel and that together build the service's value chain (Porter 1985) (Figure 7.1). The various links in that chain require both physical and nonphysical values (e.g., energy and materials and effort, and tasks and knowledge, respectively) and involve people and technologies. In addition, the provision of each service usually also relies on other internal and external values, resources and stakeholders (e.g., suppliers and supplies and other businesses as well as shareholders or governmental authorities), and the service itself is co-produced via interaction with and between other tangible and intangible values that are produced and delivered as part of a service system (Spohrer et al., 2008) (Figure 7.1). This service system is usually also part of a *service network* (i.e., system of service systems) that forms a connection between various entities and organizations to produce and deliver a service. In this scenario, the customer and the provider can use different supplies and suppliers to create a service, on the one hand, and on the other hand, they can participate in other networks (Figure 7.1). In addition, a service network is usually also part of a *value network* that defines the relationships between individuals and organizations in the generation and exchange of both tangible and intangible values, as each provider can provide various stand-alone or shared values to each customer, who consumes or co-creates separately or in conjunction with a variety of different values from other providers (Allee 2000, 2008) (Figure 7.1).

In parallel with the transformation from product dominant logic to service dominant logic, research of value networks continues to improve

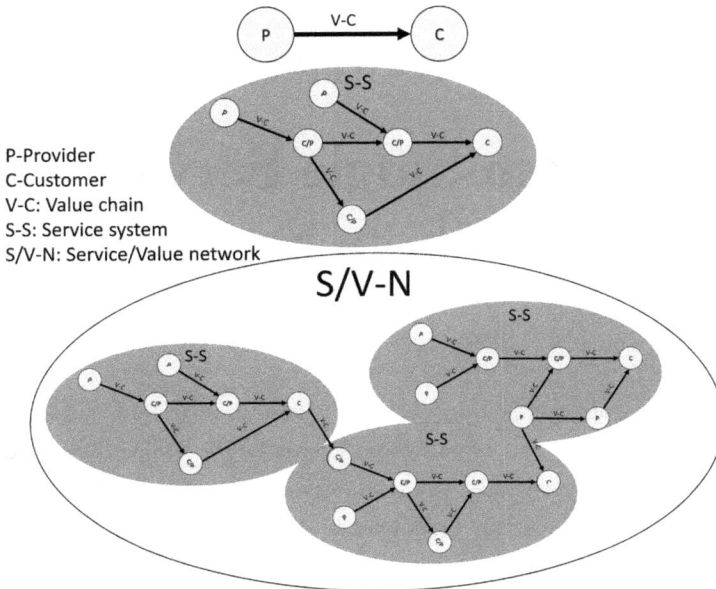

Figure 7.1 From value chain to value network

our knowledge about and understanding of them. This research has been fundamentally guided by the understanding that the traditional model of value creation via value chain is rooted in the industrial age. Today, in contrast, values are co-created in a more complex, nonlinear process that is based on the exchange of intangible values. In agreement with the sustainable service model (Chapter 2), a value network can be seen as an exchange of core-value, whether that core-value is goods or services, or a combination of the two, and that exchange generates economic-value. In turn, a value network's economic-value is generated in conjunction with a super-value that comprises knowledge and other intangible benefits, such as environmental- or social-values. These values combine to support the core-value, and all the values together serve as a medium of exchange. Allee proposed a method to map and analyze the value network with respect to three "currencies of value": (1) goods, services, and revenue (GSR); (2) knowledge; and (3) intangible benefits (Allee 2000). This method allows one to define the various players in the value network and the relationships between them while monitoring the pattern and the impact of each exchange. In addition, it can also be used to identify the most effective combinations of players and exchange patterns for imbuing the entire network with sustainable values (i.e., core- and super-value).

Recently, the related concepts of *whole service* and *holistic service systems* were introduced in the framework of service science and service dominant logic (Demirkan, Spohrer, and Krishna 2011; Spohrer 2011). Whole service can be defined as a service system or a service network that provides its customers with all the services they need, for example, a city, a luxury hotel, etc. In a closed service atmosphere, the whole service system facilitates, on the one hand, the rebuilding or the initial construction of a variety of entities, from cities to societies, and on the other hand, it can also be used to preserve old values that may still have merit. As such, the whole service system is also a good framework within which to introduce sustainability as a service, as it is equally applicable to the integration of environmental, social, and economic values within either existent or new networks.

Similar to the whole service model, the holistic service system can also support the entirety of people's needs and provide them with all the tangible and intangible values they require or want. However, the boundaries of the holistic service system extend beyond those of the whole service system, as the former deals with both the efficiency with which the various services within the whole service system are provided and the level of completeness, independence, and extended duration of the whole service system. Completeness refers to the quality of life the system delivers in terms of supplying the resources people need, developing and maintaining infrastructure and economic, health, and education systems, and implementing systems of governance. The extent to which the system does not need the support of external service systems determines its level of independence. Finally, the level of extended duration provided by a whole service can be defined for a whole service that is supplied for a short period or indefinite for whole services like smart cities. In the framework of holistic service system, therefore, the various services provided by a provider must also be interconnected, and customers must co-create the value while perpetuating the service atmosphere in the same way that ecosystem services function, thereby yielding sustainability. Thus, a sustainable service network is that which considers the whole service system and not just each individual service while sharing physical and nonphysical resources, renewing those resources in cyclical processes, and rebuilding societal infrastructure.

Examples

Value Network: E-book

Figure 7.2 illustrates e-book production and delivery as an example of a value network. The main actors and their functions in the network are: (1) customer: individuals who use the service and download the e-book, (2) provider: the web site that provides the service, (3) publisher: preparation and production of the e-book, including editing, design, etc., (4) author: the writer, (5) editor: book editing, (6) designer: book design, and (7) network company: the company that provides the network infrastructure and assistance (different companies) to the provider and the customer. This value network can be extended, of course, by adding competitor publishers and other e-book websites that influence the activity of the current publisher and provider, and customer recommendations about the provider or the book. Additional elements that the value network can incorporate that influence the entire e-book market include the overall sales figures for books and e-books, and the regulations that were implemented to define and regulate e-book market operations.

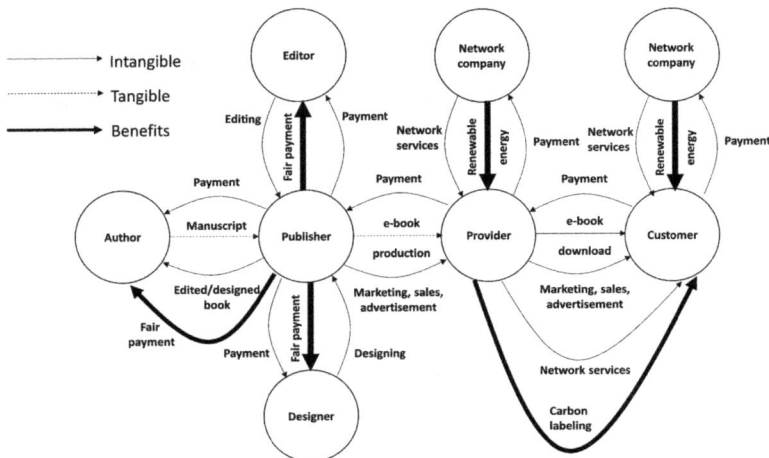

Figure 7.2 Visualization of the e-book value network

The actors in the network exchange different tangible and intangible services, some of which are illustrated in Figure 7.2. However, there are also other benefits that can be added to these interactions, such as social-values, which can include fair salary and payment conditions, and environmental-values, like reducing the environmental footprint by producing the book more efficiently, running the network company's server farm on renewable energy, and adding carbon labeling to the product or including instructions about how to perform the downloading and reading of the e-book more sustainably.

Whole Service: Smart City

The city can be seen as an example of a whole service or holistic service system in terms of the values that it generates for its customers, from citizens to visitors, to businesses, nongovernmental organizations and national or local institutions. The majority of the world's population today and a plethora of social and economic activities are concentrated in cities. Furthermore, the cities of today are not merely clusters of buildings, infrastructures, and public institutions. Instead, one of their main functions is to provide their customers with services, such as administration, maintenance, and consultation as well as the generation and provision of information. Moreover, these services are effectuated through a variety of in-house and outsourced municipal entities. Thus, to introduce sustainable-value into municipal activities, the focus on sustainability should be, in fact, on the city's services (Jones, Greenberg, and Drew 1980)

The ever-growing complexity of multimunicipal entities and systems has, in recent years, led to the need to integrate these urban operations to streamline and maximize the quality of their services, on the one hand, and, on the other, to develop processes that have more economic, social, and environmental benefits, namely, sustainable processes. To this end, the municipal service system had to be set up and rebuilt in a configuration that maximizes the value of each service separately and of all the services together, and that reconnects the city with its customers.

In general, the notion of the *sustainable city* (alternatively, *eco-city* or *green city*) refers to a city in which scientific, technical, management, and advisory activities are organized to continuously assess how the natural resource use and environmental damage associated with the city can be minimized while imposing certain limits on social and economic activities (Dempsey 2005; Kenworthy 2006; Jenks and Jones 2009). Yet a sustainable city also supplies viable alternatives to conventional models and provides new opportunities. Furthermore, a sustainable city strives to supply more efficient services in a process that yields a range of benefits and that insures its residents a higher quality of life. In recent years, however, many cities around the globe have realized that merely reducing the city's environmental impact or footprint is not enough. Accordingly, they have acknowledged that sustainability cannot be achieved without making arrangements today to counter the effects of environmental damage, including the detrimental changes we are already witnessing and those that we anticipate will occur during the lifetimes of future generations (i.e., *resilient cities*) (Godschalk 2003; Pickett, Cadenasso, and Grove 2004).

Perhaps in answer to the shortcomings of the sustainable city concept, a new strategy, termed the *smart city*, was recently introduced. The smart city integrates information and communication technologies with sustainable urban development into a comprehensive framework (Su, Li, and Fu 2011; Townsend 2013). Indeed, cities have not been immune to the technological developments of recent years, especially the information revolution, which affects every one of us on a daily basis. Many cities are therefore seeking to capitalize on these technological developments to create new ways to provide services for their residents, to continue to develop their urban spaces to increase the city's attractiveness and competitiveness, and to enhance residents' quality of life and the quality of the natural environment.

The smart city framework initially highlighted the importance of information and communication technologies and their applications in data utilization and organizational performance, all of which combine to promote more efficient decision-making processes. As such, the smart city is that which incorporates advanced technologies in the urban environment to increase the city's service performance and thus reduce the use of physical resources and costs while offering social and environmental benefits. However, despite the derivation of its name from the widespread use of advanced technology in urban centers, the notion of the smart city does not end with the implementation of technologies. Likewise, its definition is not limited to a wired, sensor filled streetscape that uses cloud computing and sophisticated software. Instead, the smart city constitutes a new conceptual framework for the development of urban space in the modern era. Moreover, it is a broad, integrated approach that aims to improve the efficiency of city operations and the quality of life of its citizens while growing its local economy and offering more integrated solutions.

To realize the goal of streamlining city operations, the smart city must coordinate the full range of urban services holistically, but this should be done while preserving the uniqueness of the city, its history and culture, and the diverse needs of all its residents. This process is driven by comprehensive, long-term planning with broad vision and the implementation of sophisticated systems of management, urban planning, and sustainable development. In addition to these, the smart city should also strive, via built-in mechanisms, to involve the public in decision-making processes and in the implementation of the city's activities while encouraging city residents to take responsibility for the space in which they live. Recruitment of the city's residents as shareholders in their city's development, in turn, leads to community empowerment to promote a healthy living environment and a high quality of life. The smart city model, therefore, needs to strike a balance between city growth and the ongoing and rapid development of technologies to preserve social- and environmental-values and leave enough space for individuals and for future generations.

The properties of the smart city are customarily divided into six major areas: (1) smart governance through democracy, transparency, and public sharing; (2) smart economy based on the local economy, green growth, and increased competitiveness; (3) smart mobility by using sophisticated transport systems and traffic management; (4) smart environment through environmental monitoring, conservation of resources, and reduction of the city's environmental footprint; (5) smart living by implementing health systems, social services, and smart homes; and (6) smart people by developing extensive education, training, and preparation programs that answer the needs of all city residents.

At the heart of the city's wisdom is the *knowledge cycle*. The first phase of this cycle is the collection of information that is stored and organized in the framework of the second stage, and then analyzed and converted into knowledge in the third stage. That knowledge is then shared and employed in the fourth stage to lead to awareness and action. The final stage and closure of the cycle comprises the application of the knowledge to create new information. The leading smart city models, however, usually allow the city to selectively distribute the knowledge it gains from the information gathered from the public and from the public domain. As such, after processing and analyzing the information, the city returns only some of the information, and occasionally also knowledge, to the general public. These models, however, are essentially flawed in that the information and knowledge obtained in the process is applied neither correctly nor optimally. Furthermore, according to these models, the municipality owns and controls the information and knowledge, despite it being rooted in data collected from the public. The role of its residents is thus reduced to that of mere consumers of information and knowledge given to them according to the policies of the municipal authority. In this scenario, the city fails to capitalize on perhaps its biggest asset of all—its citizens with their wealth of knowledge.

The city can realize the untapped potential of its residents by converting them from consumers to customers (i.e., the former take off-the-shelf municipal services without asking questions, while the latter are partners in the design and manufacture of the services). This setup can lead to the generation of a much more comprehensive database driven by better knowledge processing. Services designed and manufactured in a partnership between residents and the city, in turn, provide a wide range of extra benefits to each resident, thereby creating a smarter city. In this model, however, the cycle of information and knowledge cannot be unidirectional, namely, from the city residents to the city authorities. The smart city instead allows, and in fact encourages, its residents to gather information and produce knowledge, and then transfer it to the city and to other residents. The city's wisdom is therefore also generated in a bottom-up process, and it is not just coordinated and controlled from above by the municipal authorities. This approach has a strong potential to grow an innovative and entrepreneurial city in which information and knowledge are shared and not merely exchanged. Finally, insofar as the smart city preserves the wisdom of the past, produces knowledge in the present, and generates values for the future, its residents must be both customers and suppliers of information and knowledge, and the city has to allow residents to create their own added value. But above all, although advances in technology are integral to the smart city, technology should only be exploited as a tool and not be mistaken as the target.

In recent years, many cities around the world have implemented smart city principles, and a wide variety of projects have been executed in the public domain. Most of these new service operations are more efficient, and as such, they require fewer physical resources and generate less pollution. For example, municipal authorities have developed e-services that enable their residents and businesses to perform a variety of actions remotely from any computer or smartphone, from the payment of taxes and traffic tickets to sending complaints. The areas of transportation and traffic management have also attracted the attention of city authorities, many of whom have promoted public transport by developing faster routes for public transportation and carpool services and by issuing smart cards to its citizens that allow them to simply navigate between the means of transport and to save money in the process. To further promote public transport, a growing number of cities now limit entry by private car to their most crowded downtown areas through taxation and road rationing schemes and by establishing parking lots in strategic locations outside the cities. Singapore, for instance, launched systems that continuously monitor the movement of vehicles and road accidents in the city, and travel on all of its roads, open to the public, is priced according to a fee based on traffic congestion. By using this road pricing approach to traffic management, Singapore successfully increased mobility in the city without expanding the road network.

Another key field in which the ideas incorporated in the concept of smart cities are coming to fruition is the area of energy, where the potential applications are too numerous to count. Alongside the installation of solar systems in the public domain and computer systems to regulate street lighting, for example, also operates a sustainable neighborhood project that encourages its residents to run smart residential homes. To convert the houses to smart homes and recruit the residents as shareholders in the project, the city (1) installed smart meters that measure home energy consumption and that can be connected to devices that help residents save energy, (2) installed additional energy displays that provide feedback on energy consumption and offer personalized suggestions of how to save energy, and (3) sponsored information sessions with the neighborhood residents about saving energy while sharing useful ideas. Another city, Barcelona, installed an advanced irrigation system whose operation is based on real-time monitoring of soil moisture, and Stockholm established central fiber-optic system that enables companies operating in the city to hire local urban infrastructure communications services.

To promote the ideas discussed above, the smart city model encourages innovation and entrepreneurship among both its elected officials and its inhabitants. It allows for the implementation of novel solutions, applicable to anything ranging from public space to the residents' homes and businesses, and it promotes green growth, mainly through the development and expansion of economic opportunities while maintaining environmental quality and social justice. However, it is important to note that this model also raises several issues, especially about the complete dependence of urban systems and services on technologies as well as about ethics and individual rights violations. These issues arise in the wake of the information collection, analysis, and storage processes undertaken to generate knowledge for the public and its activities.

The main challenge facing the realization of smart cities is to transcend existing sustainability practices and defined smart city actions by striving to integrate the two. Defining smart city as a sustainable service will foster the implementation of city services, and municipal regulations and policies more sustainably while generating green growth and increasing overall quality of life. Moreover, as the majority of the resource utilization associated with the city is attributed to households and to the behavior of its citizens, the smart city should first and foremost strive to increase the co-creation of values with its citizens and allow or even oblige its customers to become providers of sustainability, both to the current generation and to those that follow. Not a trivial matter, it can be achieved by establishing the notion of sustainability as a critical perspective in the collection of data and its analysis as well as in every decision-making process. Yet it must also be based on the sharing of data and knowledge as well as on the co-creation of new sustainable values in a way that encourages and motivates all stakeholders to adopt more sustainable decision-making and solution implementation processes.

The following examples illustrate the options for adding sustainable-values to smart city operations:

1. **Sustainable big data and advanced analytics**: Smarter cities are leveraging big data and advanced analytics to improve infrastructure, planning, management, and city services with the goal of making cities more desirable, livable, sustainable, and competitive. Thus, it is important from the start to imbue the stage of data gathering and analysis with sustainability by first defining which parameters should be monitored. For example, in the field of transportation and traffic management, traffic control can be achieved not only by monitoring the number of vehicles passing a certain point per unit time, but also by assessing local air pollution and noise pollution levels and evaluating their effects on citizens.

2. **Sustainable co-creation**: Smart cities should offer services that are co-created with their residents while providing them with the opportunity and the necessary platform to be providers of sustainability in return. For example, a municipal program of waste management in smart cities should not only be limited to waste collection, sorting, and recycling, it should also promote greater social and environmental consciousness among the city's citizens. One way to achieve such added value is to educate the customers of the waste management enterprise to adopt a smart consumption culture that, in turn, will lead to a reduction in the amounts of waste generated. Similarly, smart transportation solutions should not limit their focus to traffic regulation; they should also promote public transportation and increase its use by encouraging its citizens to change their transportation habits.

3. **Share services**: The sharing of human and physical resources will beget a more socio-economic ecosystem model. In the smart city framework, information and knowledge should be shared with the city's residents to enable them to engage in more sustainable decision-making and to manage their own physical and nonphysical resources in a more sustainable fashion. For instance, a municipal

irrigation system based on the real-time monitoring of soil moisture can also deliver its data to a privately owned, computer-controlled irrigation system. However, sharing in the smart city should go beyond exchanging tangible and intangible values to include the co-production of added values with its citizens. For instance, the establishment of a community garden where citizens cooperate to grow vegetables and fruit with the assistance of the city, which provides the necessary infrastructure and training, can not only decrease the economic and environmental costs of people's groceries, it can also reconnect people with nature and promote positive community development. As such, insofar as it creates a community owned space where people meet each other on a daily basis, where educational activities are offered, and where social events can be held, the garden also fulfills an important social need. Returning to the example of transportation, the addition of organized carpooling services to the array of sustainable transportation means available in the city can also generate shared-value by allowing everyone to be a customer and/or a provider.

4. **Whole service**: A city provides its citizens or visitors with a set of services, but to introduce sustainability to this whole service requires first that services be matched and that they interact. For example, the city can create a dedicated, password protected web site with a page for each citizen where, in a one-stop solution, the city can send information and notifications, such as bills, to each customer and where the resident can perform all official interaction with the city. Another whole service opportunity is to match public transportation schedules and routes with cultural events, or to couple educational programs with a garbage reduction and waste management program.

CHAPTER 8

What Next?

From the time of the agricultural revolution through the industrial revolution and information and communication revolution and until today, the economy, which refers to the system in place for the production, distribution, and consumption of goods and services (i.e., exchange of values), has changed immeasurably at both the local and the global scales. Since antiquity, agriculture, defined as the primary sector of economy, has been the basis of life and economics. However, the industrial revolution shifted economics' center of mass to the production of goods, or the secondary sector of the economy. In general, both sectors focus on the transfer of tangible values or goods from a producer to a consumer in the sequential steps of production and delivery (i.e., goods-dominant logic). Yet the service sector, the tertiary sector of the economy, which deals with the production and delivery of intangible values, has evolved to assume a position of dominance in world economics (i.e., service dominant logic), and the growth of the service sector also changed the proportions and interrelations between other sectors of the economy, such as rural and urban, public and private and domestic- and export-oriented. Moreover, the new generation of services has totally changed the arrangement of resources and their division between provider and customer. For instance, while Facebook is the world's most popular social media website, it creates no content; Uber and Airbnb, which are the largest taxi and accommodation companies in the world, respectively, own no vehicles or rooms; and Alibaba is a huge retail company with no inventory.

As systems will inevitably continue to evolve as they adapt to the changing needs of people and the world we live in, what forms will the next generation of tangible and intangible values exchange and co-creation take? Are we on the edge of a new revolution? If so, what new technology will usher in this revolution?

Though some would say that the prophecy has been given to fools, current technological as well as environmental, social, and economic changes hint at the answers to these questions. In general, it is agreed that every revolution is based on technological breakthroughs that reorganize the socio-economic order. In addition, throughout history, three main elements—energy, transportation, and communication—have been recognized as the drivers of every revolution. Thus the industrial revolution, fueled by coal and the steam engine, gave way to trains, boats, and the telegraph with the beginning of capitalism, which fostered the developments of gasoline and electricity, private vehicles and the telephone during the 20th century. These, in turn, facilitated the development of television, radio, and the Internet later. In his latest book *The Zero Marginal Cost Society*, futurologist Jeremy Rifkin revealed that the next revolution will encompass everything from the computerized world to the physical world such that we will be able to "copy and paste" everything, including physical items (Rifkin 2014). This revolution will be based on (1) Internet communication, which will enable and promote both "Internet of Things" (Weber and Weber 2010; Xia et al., 2014) and "Internet of Energy" (Davies 2010; Bui et al., 2012); and on (2) widely available and affordable 3D printers that will be simple and cheap to use and that will allow people to self-produce their own goods for their consumption. In this scenario, the need to physically deliver and transport products will be rendered almost obsolete. Taken together, these changes, Rifkin claims, will yield a new regime known as the *creative commons* (Rifkin 2014).

The Internet of Things (IoT) is the network of physical objects where communication between the objects is driven by specialized electronics, software, and sensors that are embedded in them. In this approach, insofar as "things" can collect and exchange data, they can also be remotely controlled in a system that intensifies the integration not only of the physical and virtual worlds, but also of tangible and intangible values. An already well-established example of IoT comprises the control of domestic electronic devices by smartphones and similar devices. Furthermore, this integrated and dynamic network infrastructure will form connections between the energy network and the Internet to streamline the generation, storage, and flow of energy (i.e., Internet of Energy).

Based on current forecasts, services will continue to play an important role in the next and subsequent revolutions. From the perspectives of service dominant logic and service science, therefore, the near future will witness the developments of four main concepts:

1. *Value in-return:* In contrast to the finiteness and perishability of physical resources, nonphysical resources are not limited, at least not in the foreseeable future, indicating that information and knowledge can be expanded indefinitely. Nevertheless, nonphysical resources should also be used and managed rationally. Similar to physical resources, therefore, they should be reused, recycled, and recovered to promote process efficiency today, on the one hand, and to ensure, on the other hand, that future processes will be defined by the same values. Thus, service provision, which is based on the co-creation of an intangible core-value by provider and customer, should also promote the reuse and recycling of the value while recruiting both provider and customer to *co-generate* values for other stakeholders (i.e., super-value).

2. *Self-production of goods:* Although today self-services are ubiquitous, the self-production of one's goods that was once a necessity for survival was expropriated from individuals, first by farmers with the advent of the agricultural revolution, and later by the ability to mass produce goods, as a result of the Industrial Revolution. But the classic industrial model advanced by the Industrial Revolution, according to which the majority of the knowledge and technologies exploited in the manufacture of synthetic products is typically owned by companies, is gradually being modified and replaced. Recent advances in technology have engendered the ability of almost everyone to produce myriad goods by themselves using easily accessible, domestic equipment. Moreover, this inherently generative process will further advance the service sector, because these new technologies and production processes also require supporting and complementary services.

3. *Internet of Things:* Internet-based services will be used not just for communication between human beings and computers to generate intangible values, but also to create connections between people and goods as well as between goods themselves.

4. *3D Services:* As service systems and value networks will continue to expand and develop while accounting for different actors (e.g., providers, customers, suppliers, and stakeholders) and values (e.g., environmental, social, and economic), services will have to be designed, produced, and delivered in three dimensions. 3D services are those that combine various levels of value directions (i.e., provision of value in-exchange, co-creation of value in-use, and co-generation of value in-return) while considering the economic, environmental, and social components of each value.

Value In-Return

Over the years, the characterization of service in the framework of service dominant logic has evolved, and the roles of the producer, the client, and other actors involved in the production and delivery of the value have changed accordingly (Vargo and Lush 2008). Originally, service was defined according to the value in-exchange model as the transfer of an intangible value from a producer to a client. In this model, the design and generation of the value is solely the responsibility of the producer, which invests in all the physical and nonphysical resources relevant to provision of the service. Included among these resources are materials and energy, facilities, effort and information, and knowledge. The producer also delivers the value to the client, who simultaneously uses it, as expressed by the notion of service inseparability, and pays for it in exchange. The value is thus produced and delivered in two separate, sequential steps that resemble the production and delivery of goods (Table 8.1-entry 1). In addition, both the producer and the client have distinct roles: the producer acts as a supplier that generates and distributes the value and manages the supply chain, while the client is actually a consumer. Throughout this process, the value flows in one direction.

Besides shifting the fundamental basis of exchange from tangible to intangible values, the service dominant logic approach also marked a change in marketing, such that company preferences shifted from marketing *to* their consumers to marketing *with* their customers. It thus redefined value exchange in the framework of a value in-use model and focused on the value co-creation process. According to the value in-use model, a value is jointly and reciprocally created by the producer and

Table 8.1 *Characteristics of different service models*

Entry	Producer	Value	Client	Interactions	Value direction*	Responsibility and control*
1	Supplier	In-exchange	Consumer	none	From S to C	S
2	Provider	In-use	Customer	Co-creation	From P to C	S and C
3	Providers	In-context	Customer	Co-creation	from Ps to C	S and C
4	Provider and Enabler	In-return	Customer and Provider	Co-generation	From E to C/P and to Cs	Mainly C

*S = supplier; C = customer; P = provider; E = enabler

the client. Moreover, the model also accounts for the interactions among all beneficiaries via the integration of resources and the implementation of competences (Table 8.1-entry 2) (Vargo, Maglio, and Akaka 2008). In addition, the notion of co-creation from the value in-use perspective also divided the resources and capabilities relevant to the service between the producer and the client and changed the corresponding roles played by the two sides in the production and transformation of the value. In fact, it turned the supplier into a provider that, besides investing resources and capabilities, also provides the consumer with a platform allowing the latter to become actively involved in the value production and delivery process, thereby becoming a customer. The value co-creation process also emphasized another characteristic of service: its inconsistency, which reflects the wide variability of any service and the fact that the delivery of a service cannot be repeated in exactly the same way, as the provider, the customer, and the place and time of delivery change from one instance of service to the next. In this scenario, however, the value is still delivered in one direction, from the provider to the customer. Finally, Chandler and Vargo (2011) argued that to provide more specific and accurate value, the time, the place, and the requirement as well as abilities of the relevant actors (i.e., provider, co-providers, and customer) should be integrated and synchronized. Thus they offered a new model of value proposition, named *value in-context* (Table 8.1-entry 3), that assigns more responsibility in the co-creation process to the customer, who should control the creation and delivery of the value in a given situation.

The rapid growth in service science research and development dictates that we reconsider how services are produced and delivered and what roles the provider, the customer, and other actors in the process play. Moreover, this reassessment must also take into account the economy and marketing trends and the relevant social and environmental implications. Therefore, we recently offered a novel perspective on sustainable services that depicts service as the integration of a core-value, which represents the purpose and essence of the service, with a super-service, which includes other supportive or complementary intangible values associated with the service (Wolfson et al., 2010, 2015). According to this model of sustainable services, the provider allows and even encourages the customer to become a co-provider of sustainability as a super-value to both the current and next generations. In addition, the co-creation process is driven by multiple customers, including direct and indirect customers who should participate, either actively or inactively, in the process

The joint generation and delivery of a super-value by the customer and the provider to subsequent customers is not limited to sustainability or social justice. The core-value can also be regenerated from the customer to the provider, after which it can be co-generated and delivered by both, and then used by other direct customers or stakeholders. This co-generation process, termed *value in-return*, progressively recruits additional customers to the service and also transforms customers into co-providers (Figure 8.1, Table 8.1-entry 4). Yet value in-return does not signify merely the assignment of another role or new tasks to the customer or the transfer of a part of the value from the customer to the provider and their co-generation of a new value to be delivered to other customers. This new paradigm dictates that as the value must be returned, the involvement

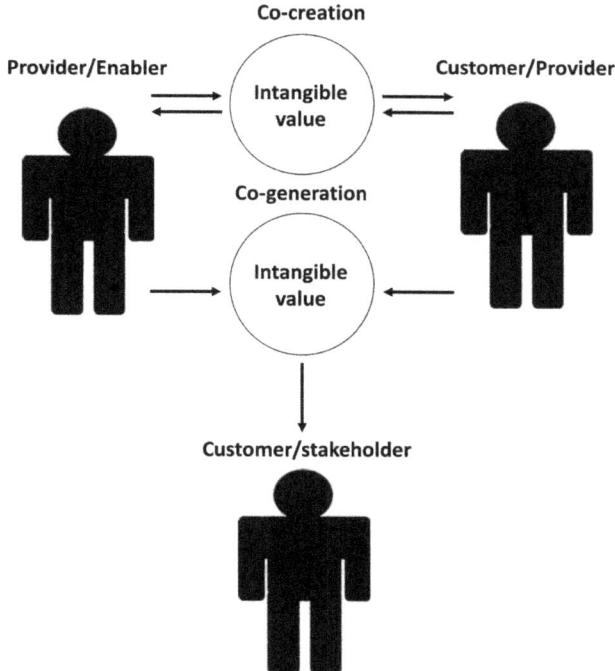

Figure 8.1 Value in-return model

of the customer as a co-provider in the co-creation and use of the original value must also change. Furthermore, the value in-return approach also forces the provider to create a platform for the co-generation process to enable the customer to return a value. The provider thus assumes the role of enabler while the customer, who is simultaneously also a provider, actually has more responsibility for the co-generation of the value and correspondingly greater responsibility for the process as a whole. Finally, these changes in the roles, attitudes, and skills of both the provider and the customer alter the entire value generation and delivery process, which may ultimately result in the generation of a value that differs considerably from the original value of the service. Under the value in-return model, therefore, the co-generation of services not only has the potential to make services more efficient and productive, it also creates new opportunities for entrepreneurship and innovation in the services sector.

Indeed, opportunities for innovation in the service sector abound. Insofar as a service provides an intangible solution to a customer's particular need or want, how providers and customers design, create, deliver, and use a service is usually guided by these needs. As such, services are increasingly tailored to the different requirements of each customer. In contrast to the generic nature of value in-exchange services, which are designed for one type of consumer, value in-use services offer a more customer centric approach that distinguishes between the nuanced differences in the needs and abilities of its different customers while recruiting their skills to create and deliver the value. These changes also compel customers to adapt not only their service consumption habits, but also, more broadly, their lifestyles. Likewise, the design, generation, delivery, and use of a service from the value in-return perspective is expected to effect similar changes, both in how customers consume services and in consumer lifestyles. However, because customers also become co-providers, how they co-generate value is also expected to change their consumption habits and their value co-creation and co-generation practices

Examples

Today's social networks and information and communication technologies foster broad operational leeway for value co-generation in the framework of the value in-return model. Take, for example, a carpooling service: the car may be owned solely by one of the service's users, jointly by some of the passengers, or by a cooperative or a company, and each user of the service can be a driver or a passenger (i.e., a provider or a customer, respectively). Moreover, the sharing platform used in this service, whether an Internet site or a WhatsApp group, enables its users to co-generate the service and return the value. The same dual customer-provider role can also be found in the joint operations of cooperatives, which are associations of people who cooperate for their mutual benefit. Another service, Waze, a community-based traffic and navigation application, simultaneously enables every user to be a customer who uses the platform for his or her navigation and a provider who co-generates and delivers a value to other customers using the Waze platform. In this example, the return of the core-value to the system by the customer transforms the latter into a co-provider.

The value in-return model is also a viable framework for the co-generation of a super-value by a provider and a customer in the production and delivery of a service to another customer. For instance, a service that finds matches between customer needs and the professionals with the relevant qualifications can provide its customers with the opportunity to give feedback that will, in turn, help the provider co-create a better value with subsequent customers.

The differences between each service model and the opportunities that they offer can be highlighted by an analysis of the production and delivery of a representative value such as flight reservations. In a traditional value in-exchange model, the client, in a person-to-person mode, enlists the aid of a supplier, typically a travel agency, to book a flight and reserve a seat on the plane, and the supplier sends the ticket to the consumer. Alternatively, in a value in-use model, the flight company is the provider, and it sets up an Internet platform for the co-creation of a service in self-service mode, in which customers search for and book flights for themselves. In addition, because commercial flights are known to emit large amounts of greenhouse gases, the provider of the flight reservation service can also offer its customers a complementary super-value to enable the customers offset the emissions associated with their flights. In this scenario, customers could be offered the option of paying an extra fee, such as a certain amount per kilometer, which will be invested in an environmental foundation, the planting of new trees, or the development of clean energies. This value is actually co-generated by the provider and the customer, who becomes a co-provider, and together they deliver a service to other customers. Moreover, the offsetting of greenhouse gas emissions delivers sustainability both to the present and the next generations. Similarly, trip accommodations can be ordered through a travel agency or directly from the hotel in a value in-exchange mode or, alternatively, in a value in-use mode, using a hotel's Internet site or a dedicated Internet site, such as Booking, Agoda or Trivago. In addition, the value can also be generated via a value in-return mode in which the customer re-generates a super-value by, for example, rating the hotel or writing a review. Alternatively, the Airbnb site offers a value in-return platform, where the customer can book a room and, either simultaneously or in a separate action, offer a room.

As previously noted, a value in-return mode approach to service co-generation can also function as a platform to alter how we consume or co-create services and marketing. For instance, people whose transportation needs cannot be met by a public transit service due to the service's schedule and/or route may resort to using their private cars or attempt to change the schedule. But viable alternative is that they try to change their schedules to fit that of the service, which generates value in-return, as the customer uses the service and does not search for an alternative. For this type of value in-return to work, however, not only customer willingness to adopt different behavior is needed, but also needed is the design of more efficient and rational services.

Self-Production

The self-production of goods, already technologically possible, can be performed by almost everyone today. For example, 3D printers allow a variety of goods to be printed at home using a simple process and at a reasonable price. Although the currently available domestic 3D printers are themselves still relatively expensive and are capable of producing objects from a limited number of types of plastic, 3D printer technology is developing rapidly, and prices are therefore expected to decline. In addition, although the production and delivery stages of self-production with 3D printers are performed at home, self-production does not eliminate the need to extract raw materials or the need to outsource the end-of-life phase of the good's life cycle to ensure optimal resource recovery and recycling.

Food entails another opportunity for self-production, but in this case, the entire life cycle, from cradle-to-cradle, is under self-production. Nonetheless, large areas of land and significant infrastructure are required for food production, rendering it unsuitable in crowded cities. But replacing the greengrocer with a farmer who customers buy from directly can eliminate the need for intermediaries, such as a shipping company, increase the quality of the fruits and vegetables, and reduce their price.

In general, self-production technologies are expected to decentralize the goods manufacturing process, which will result in substantially lower prices, as the technology will eliminate the delivery stage of the life cycle and avoid the role of any intermediary entity. Domestic self-production technologies are also derived from the desire and even the need of individuals to be unique. However, it is too early to determine whether the self-production mode, which transforms everyone into a *prosumer* (i.e., a combination of producer and consumer), will constitute the next generation of the industrial revolution, which could also mark a return to a market driven by the goods dominant logic.

As goods delivery is also associated with the provision of different services during the whole good's life cycle, the self-production of goods is also expected to change the types of services that will be required for this process to develop. For example, while the delivery stage of the life cycle will almost vanish (e.g., marketing, sales, transportation, and other services), alternative services that support the production stage of a good's life cycle, such as goods design and device maintenance, will be required. Moreover, self-production will allow everyone to be not only a producer of goods for his or her own use, but also become a provider of goods to others. It will thus also involve the co-creation of various sharing services, from the barter of goods and machine rental to the exchange of services and the joint production of goods and service, and as such, it is expected to develop the local economy.

In the frame of sustainability, the self-production of goods is expected to revolutionize our consumption habits. On the one hand, as production will be simple, accessible, and cheap, self-production may result in the over-production of goods (i.e., rebound effect), thereby reducing the life time of goods to an even greater extent than today. On the other hand, as every prosumer can "feel" or sense the amounts of resources and the requirements that were invested in the production of each good, self-production could also lead to more conscientious consumption. Furthermore, the ability to produce a one-of-a-kind product can result in the production of goods and services conforming to specific customer needs and lead to the more intensive use of each item.

The age of self-production, however, should not repeat the mistakes it was designed to rectify, namely, the abuse of the Earth's limited natural resources. As the driving force behind the depletion of physical resources, our espousal and embracement of the good dominant logic led to the severe degradation of the natural environment that currently impinges on its ability to maintain ecosystem services and renew resources. Thus, besides the coupling of goods and services (i.e., product-service system) and the integration of CleanServs with each good's life cycle stage, self-processes can be made more sustainable by imbuing self-production processes with more soul, consciousness, and morals. In parallel, social and environmental values that account for the long-term and broad effects of the process must also be introduced. To do so, self-production processes should be performed under a service orientation, in which the notion of the service's intangibility, perishability, inseparability, and heterogeneity is considered. One of the first steps in this process, and indeed, integral to its success, is the transformation of people from prosumers, a role that only combines the roles of producer and consumer in one entity but that preserves the notion of consumerism, to *provomers* (i.e., a combination of provider and customers).

A novel role developed within the self-production framework, the concept of the provomer entails greater responsibility not only toward the production process, but also toward the whole life cycle of the product (e.g., product recycling should be an imperative). The co-creation and co-generation of values in-use and in-return by a provomer can lead, in turn, to lower prices, the rational use of resources, and more environmentally friendly production processes. In addition, the provomer framework will also allow and encourage the sharing of unused resources and assets (e.g., production of goods not for self-use). Insofar as this role incorporates both provider and customer, the provomer should therefore be engaged in a self-co-creation process. Thus, the sustainable division of resources and tasks from this perspective should be conceptual, in that the provomer seeks to balance between the use-value and the exchange-value of each self-produced good. For the provomer, that balance should be between the costs of the raw materials for the production of the product, to its use and the burden that use has on the social and natural environments. Hence, in self-production mode, the producer who functions as a provider should ask whether production of the item is beneficial and justifiable, while the consumer who has become a customer should evaluate whether purchase and use of the product is worthy. Under self-production, therefore, the two typically sequential steps of production and delivery in the good's life cycle should be coupled into a single step as with a service.

Internet of Things

The Internet of Things (IoT) describes an interconnection of technologies in a system comprising people, physical objects, and information technologies. It actually refers to the servicizing of products, but with one significant difference from product-service systems: the direct provider and customer are "things" and not people. In addition, the IoT enables better servicizing and greater system uptime, increases efficiency and accessibility, and achieves higher output with lower input, thereby increasing the value of all connected things. Moreover, rather than just flowing through the value chain, the product actually assumes an active role and participates in the value chain. At last, the IoT also entails new opportunities to create whole services and holistic service systems, such as smart cities.

From a sustainability perspective, a major challenge entailed in "things" is expressed in the pursuit of a balance between an underuse of the resources and assets consumed during the pre-use stages of the good's life cycle and an excess use of goods (i.e., rebound effect). This goal can be facilitated by adding the ability to collect and exchange data between devices, a powerful tool that can provide people with valuable information about the real performance of each product and about the actual needs people have and how they use their products. The seamless collection and exchange of data will thus increase the efficiency with which "things" are used in, for example, educating customers in how to most effectively use a good or offering different good's sharing mechanisms. It will also enable anyone to know the condition of a product—whether it functions properly or it needs to be fixed, and even which, if any of its components can be reused before disposal. Furthermore, information and system intelligence can be exploited to accelerate sustainable development, as it allows real time analyses to be run on process and product performances, thus allowing the environmental-values of "things" to be managed and controlled. Yet as sustainability is about more from less, the IoT should not be just about running processes more efficiently or using fewer resources, it should also be about implementing change. It should introduce products and services with new environmental-values, such as turning off a device or a process when the threat or risk to the environment is high or managing traffic according to prevalent situations. In addition to environmental-values, new social-values should be integral to products and services. These could be improvements in the co-creation of healthcare, education, and social services, for instance, allowing a pacemaker to be controlled remotely (Vermesan and Friess 2011).

Finally, as the IoT is about the "humanization" of "things", these smart entities being actors in service systems or value networks, there is also room to add other nonhuman actors to the network, such as nature, animals, and plants, both as providers and as customers. In this way, these actors will also be able to take part in value co-creation and co-generation processes, and in so doing, they will obtain their rightful places in the overall scheme and preserve their rights. The addition of other nonhuman actors will also add corresponding sustainable-values to the network. However, even though both provider and customer are "things" in the IoT, the generation and adoption of values is always initiated (and sometimes terminated) by people. The whole value should therefore be viewed holistically. Finally, it seems that it is not enough to match services to goods life cycles or goods to service life cycles, but instead, it is now necessary to match the two life cycles to one.

3D Services

Service systems and networks will undoubtedly become much more complex and specific in the future, and as such, they will require better coordination of the various actors, whether human or not, and better synchronization of the value production and delivery processes. 3D services comprise three levels: (1) unidirectional value exchange from supplier to consumer, (2) bidirectional value co-creation between provider and customer, and (3) return of values by simultaneous co-generation of direct and indirect values by a provider and a customer to other customers.

The development of 3D services must be done with the goal of imbuing the service production and delivery processes with sociotechnical dimensions (i.e., to connect people with technology [Carayon 2006]) while increasing the suitability of the service system for human use and experience (i.e., the human side of service engineering [HSSE] [Freund and Cellary 2014]). A primary goal, and indeed, requirement, of that process will be the production of wise values, and these must permeate the entire value hierarchy (i.e., DIKIW-data, information, knowledge, intelligence, and wisdom [Ackoff 1989, Spohrer et al., 2016]). The creation of wise values will begin with the collection of raw data that is communicated and then processed into information that can eventually be utilized to improve decision-making and generate more knowledge. This knowledge can then be invested in intelligent solutions that increase process efficiency and, in the end, generate wisdom that increase effectiveness. In short, a wise value is that which strikes a balance between individual and collective human values while having a positive impact on future generations (Spohrer et al., 2016).

Finally, shifting from the 2D to the 3D model will enable the provision of long-term and indirect values and the co-creation of values with many indirect actors and even with the next generations. Moreover, this 3D model will be based on the generation of environmental, social and economic values integrated into the provision of sustainability as a value. Finally, this model also resembles the provision of ecosystem services, which combine and integrate production and delivery with provision, regulation, and supporting services.

References

Ackoff, R.L. 1989. "From data to wisdom." *Journal of Applied Systems Analysis* 16:3–9.

Ager, A.K., M. Lembani, A. Mohammed, G.M. Ashir, A. Abdulwahab, H. de Pinho, and Zarowsky, C. 2015. "Health service resilience in Yobe state, Nigeria in the context of the Boko Haram insurgency: A systems dynamics analysis using group model building." *Conflict and Health* 9(1):1–14.

Allee, V. 2000. "Reconfiguring the value network." *Journal of Business strategy* 21(4):36–9.

Allee, V. 2008. "Value network analysis and value conversion of tangible and intangible assets." *Journal of Intellectual Capital* 9(1):5–24.

Allen, R. 1980. *How to save the world: Strategy for world conservation.* London: Kogan Page Ltd.

Alter, S. 2008. "Service system fundamentals: Work system, value-chain, and life cycle." *IBM Systems Journal* 47:71–85.

Andersen, M.S. 2007. "An introductory note on the environmental economics of the circular economy." *Sustainability Science* 2(1):133–40.

Barker, G. 2009. *The Agricultural Revolution in Prehistory: Why did Foragers become Farmers?* Oxford: Oxford University Press.

Berkhout, P.H., J.C. Muskens, and J.W. Velthuijsen. 2000. "Defining the rebound effect." *Energy Policy* 28(6):425–32.

Berners-Lee, M. 2015. "How bad are bananas?" Fifth assessment report of the UN's Intergovernmental Panel on Climate Change, McAfee study Carbon Footprint of Spam.

Botsman, R., and R. Rogers. 2011. *What's mine is yours: How collaborative consumption is changing the way we live.* London: Collins.

Bowen, H.R. 1953. *Social responsibility of the businesses.* New York: Harper and Row.

Brezet, J.C., A.S. Bijma, J. Ehrenfeld, and S. Silvester. 2001. *The design of eco-efficient services.* Delft University of Technology, Design for Sustainability Program.

Brundtland, G., M. Khalid, S. Agnelli, S. Al-Athel, B. Chidzero, L. Fadika, V. Hauff, I. Lang, M. Shijun, M.M. de Botero, and M. Singh. 1987. "Our Common Future." World Commission on Environmental Development.

Bui, N., A.P. Castellani, P. Casari, and M. Zorzi. 2012. "The Internet of energy: A web-enabled smart grid system." *Network, IEEE* 26(4):39–45.

Cabanatuan, M. 2010. "BART can't keep pace with rising 'crush loads'." *SFGate*. http://m.sfgate.com/bpm_test/article/BART-can-t-keep-pace-with-rising-crush-loads-6234574.php (2.1.2016).

Campbell, C.S., P.P. Maglio, and M. Davis. 2011. "From self-service to super-service: How to shift the boundary between customer and provider." *Information System and E-Business Management* 9:173–91.

Carayon, P. 2006. "Human factors of complex sociotechnical systems." *Applied Ergonomics* 37(4):525–35.

Chaffee, C., and B.R. Yaros. 2000. "Life cycle assessment for three types of grocery bags—recyclable plastic; compostable, biodegradable plastic; and recycled, recyclable paper." Boustead Consulting & Associates Ltd. www.heartland.org/sites/default/files/threetypeofgroceryb ags.pdf (2.1.2016).

Chandler, J.D., and S.L. Vargo. 2011. "Contextualization and value-in-context: How context frames exchange." *Marketing Theory* 11(1):5–49.

Chester, M.V., and H. Arpad. 2009. "Environmental assessment of passenger transportation should include infrastructure and supply chains." *Environmental Research Letter* 4(2):1–8.

Chouinard, Y., J. Ellison, and R. Ridgeway. 2011. "The sustainable economy." *Harvard Business Review* 89(10):52–62.

Clark, J.M. 1916. "The changing basis of economic responsibility." *Journal of Political Economy* 24(3): 218–24.

Clark, J.M. 1939. *Social Control of Business*, 2nd ed. New York: McGraw-Hill.

Cohen, M.A., and M.P. Vandenbergh. 2012. "The potential role of carbon labeling in a green economy." *Energy Economics* 34:S53–S63.

Costanza, R., B.G. Norton, and B.D. Haskell. 1992. *Ecosystem health: New goals for environmental management*. Washington DC: Island Press.

Davies, S. 2010. "Internet of Energy." *Engineering & Technology* 16(5):42–5.

Day, G.S. 1981. "The product life cycle: Analysis and applications issues." *The Journal of Marketing* 45(4):60–7.

de Chernatony, L., F. Harris, and F. Dall'Olmo Riley. 2000. "Added value: Its nature, roles and sustainability." *European Journal of Marketing* 34(1/2):39–56.

Demirkan, H., J.C. Spohrer, and V. Krishna (eds). 2011. "Service and science." *The Science of Service Systems.* New York: Springer.

Dempsey, N. 2005. *Future forms and design for sustainable cities.* Oxford: Routledge.

DeSimone, L.D., and F. Popoff. 2000. Eco-efficiency: The business link to sustainable development. Massachusetts: MIT Press.

Downes, J., B. Thomas, and H. Walker. 2011. "Longer product lifetimes." Limited report for Defra on Extended Product Lifetimes.

Dresner, S. 2008. *The principles of sustainability,* 2nd ed. Oxford: EarthScan.

Edvardsson, B., B. Tronvoll, and T. Gruber. 2011. "Expanding understanding of service exchange and value co-creation: A social construction approach." *Journal of the Academy of Marketing Science* 39(2):327–39.

Edwards, A.R. 2005. *The sustainability revolution: Portrait of a paradigm shift.* Gabriola Island: New Society Publishers.

Elkington, J. 2004. "Enter the triple bottom line." In *The triple bottom line: Does it all add up*, ed. A. Henriques, and J. Richardson. New York: Earthescan.

Felson, M., and J.L. Spaeth. 1978. "Community structure and collaborative consumption: A routine activity approach." *American Behavioral Scientist* 21:614–24.

Finnveden, G., M.Z. Hauschild, T. Ekvall, J. Guinée, R. Heijungs, S. Hellweg, and S. Suh. 2009. "Recent developments in life cycle assessment." *Journal of Environmental Management* 91(1):1–21.

Fitzsimmons, J.A., and M.J. Fitzsimmons. 2006. *Service management: operations, strategy, and information technology*, 5th ed. Boston: McGraw-Hill.

Foster, J.B., and E.M. Wood. 1997. *Capitalism and the information age: The political economy of the global communication revolution.* New York: Monthly Review Press.

Freund, L., and Wojciech Cellary. 2014. *Advances in the human side of service engineering.* AHFE Conference.

Friedman, B., and P.H. Kahn Jr. 2002. "Human values, ethics, and design." In *The human-computer interaction handbook*, ed. A. Sears, and J.A. Jacko. L. Mahwah: Erlbaum Associates Inc. pp. 1177–201.

Garcia, A. 2013. "Resource efficiency indicators for EU product policy-Embedded energy in washing machines." www.eeb .org/?LinkServID=A2CE255D-5056-B741-DBDDC31BFB 821E13&showMeta=0&aa, (2.1.16).

Gibbins, P. 1976. "Use-value and exchange-value." Theory and Decision 7(3):171–9.

Godschalk, D. R. 2003. "Urban hazard mitigation: Creating resilient cities." *Natural Hazards Review* 4(3): 136–43.

Goedkoop, M.J., J.G. van Halen, H. te Riele, and P.J.M. Rommens. 1999. *Product-service systems, ecological and economic basics*. Ministry of Environment, The Hague, Netherlands.

Google green. www.google.co.il/green/bigpicture/#/, (2.1.16).

Gretchen, C.D. 1997. *Nature's services, societal dependence on natural ecosystems*. Washington, D.C.: Island Press.

Grunert, K.G., S. Hieke, and J. Wills. 2014. "Sustainability labels on food products: Consumer motivation, understanding and use." *Food Policy* 44:177–89.

Guenther, M., C.M. Saunders, and P.R. Tait. 2012. "Carbon labeling and consumer attitudes." *Carbon Management Journal* 3(5):445–55.

Hall, T. 1995. "The second industrial revolution: Cultural reconstructions of industrial regions." *Landscape Research* 20(3):112–23.

Heinrichs, H. 2013. "Sharing economy: A potential new pathway to sustainability." *Gaia: Ecological Perspectives for Science & Society* 22(4):228.

Hu, A.H., R.W. Lin, C. Y. Huang, and C.L. Wu. 2012. "Carbon reduction assessment of a product service system: A case study of washing machines." In *Design for Innovative Value Towards a Sustainable Society*. New York: Springer.

Humphrey, C., and S. Hugh-Jones. 1992. *Barter, exchange and value: An anthropological approach*. Cambridge: Cambridge University Press.

Huppes, G., and M. Ishikawa. 2007. *Quantified Eco-Efficiency*. New York: Springer.

Jeffery, M.I. 2005. "Environmental ethics and sustainable development: Ethical and human rights issues in implementing Indigenous rights." *Macquarie Journal of International and Comparative Environmental Law* 2:105.

Jenks, M., and C. Jones. 2009. *Dimensions of the sustainable city* (Vol. 2). New York: Springer Science & Business Media.

IBM Almaden Services Research. 2006. "Service science, management, and engineering (SSME): Challenges, frameworks, and call for participation." San Jose: IBM Almaden Research Center, Almaden Research Center.

Jones, B. D., S. Greenberg, and J. Drew. 1980. *Service delivery in the city: Citizen demand and bureaucratic rules.* Longman Publishing Group.

Karr, J.R., and D.R. Dudley. 1981. "Ecological perspective on water quality goals." *Environmental Management* 5(1):55–68.

Kennedy, C., S. Pincetl, and P. Bunje. 2011. "The study of urban metabolism and its applications to urban planning and design." *Environmental Pollution* 159(8):1965–73.

Kenworthy, J., and F. Laube. 2001. "The millennium cities database for sustainable transport." *International Association of Public Transport,* Belgium.

Kenworthy, J.R. (2006). "The eco-city: Ten key transport and planning dimensions for sustainable city development." *Environment and urbanization* 18(1): 67–85.

Kloepffer, W. 2008. "Life cycle sustainability assessment of products." *The International Journal of Life Cycle Assessment* 13(2):89–95.

Kreps, T.J. 1940. "Measurement of the social performance of businesses." Monograph no. 7, *An in investigation of concentration of economic power for the Temporary National Economic Committee,* Washington. DC, USA.

Kwak, T.J., and M.C. Freeman. 2010. "Assessment and management of ecological integrity." In *Inland fisheries management in North America,* 3rd ed. eds. W.A. Hubert and M.C. Quist. Bethesda, Maryland: American Fisheries Society.

Leake, J., and R. Woods. 2009. "Revealed: The environmental impact of Google searches." *The Sunday Times.* www.thesundaytimes.co.uk/sto/ingear/tech_and_net/article142550.ece (2.1.2016).

Leismann, K., M. Schmitt, H. Rohn, and C. Baedeker. 2013. "Collaborative consumption: Towards a resource-saving consumption culture." *Resources* 2(3):184–203.

Litman, T. 2007. "Developing indicators for comprehensive and sustainable transport planning." *Transportation Research Record: Journal of the Transportation Research Board*, 10–15.

Lu, Y., R. Wang, Y. Zhang, H. Su, P. Wang, A. Jenkins, and G. Squire. 2015. "Ecosystem health towards sustainability." *Ecosystem Health and Sustainability* 1(1):1–15.

Lucas, R.E. 2002. *Lectures on economic growth.* Massachusetts: Harvard University Press.

Lusch R.F., and S.L. Vargo. 2006. *The service-dominant logic of marketing: dialog, Debate, and Directions.* New York: M.E. Sharpe Inc.

Maglio, P. P., and J.C. Spohrer. 2007. *Fundamentals of service science.* San Jose: IBM

Maglio, P.P., C.A. Kieliszewski, and J.C. Spohrer. 2010. *Handbook of Service Science.* New York: Springer.

Meade, J.E. 1986. *Different forms of share economy.* Public Policy Centre.

Mellars, P.A., and C. Stringer. 1989. *The human revolution. Behavioral and biological perspectives in the origins of modern humans.* Edinburgh: Edinburgh University Press.

Miles, S. 1998. *Consumerism: as a way of life.* Thousand Oaks: Sage Publication.

Moura-Leite, R.C., and R.C. Padgett. 2011. "Historical background of corporate social responsibility." *Social Responsibility Journal* 7(4): 528–39.

Narayanaswamy, V., J.A. Scott, J.N. Ness, and M. Lochhead. 2003. "Resource flow and product chain analysis as practical tools to promote cleaner production initiatives." *Journal of Cleaner Production* 11(4): 375–87.

Nash, R.F. 1989. *The rights of nature: a history of environmental ethics.* Wisconsin: University of Wisconsin Press.

NHS Sustainable development unit. 2010. "Saving carbon, improving health." NHS carbon reduction strategy update 2010.

Nielsen, K.S. 2015. "Can a carbon label influence consumers' purchasing behavior on coffee?" Aarhus University School of Business and Social Science.

Ning, D. 2001. "Cleaner production, eco-industry and circular economy." *Research of Environmental Science* 6:1–4.

Normann, R., R. Ramírez. 1993. "From value chain to value constellation: designing interactive strategy." *Harvard Business Review* 71(4):65–77.

Odum, E.P., H.T. Odum, and J. Andrews. 1971. *Fundamentals of Ecology* (Vol. 3). Philadelphia: Saunders.

O'Riordan, T. 1995. *Environnemental science for environnemental management.* New York: Longman Group Limited.

Owens, J.W. 1997. "Life cycle assessment." *Journal of Industrial Ecology* 1(1):37–49.

Pernick, R, and C. Wilder. 2007. *The clean tech revolution: the next big growth and investment opportunity.* New York: Harper-Collins Publishers.

Pickett, S., M. Cadenasso, and Morgan Groove. 2004. "Resilient cities: Meaning, models, and metaphors for integrating the ecological, socio-economic, and planning realms." *Landscape and Urban Planning* 69:369–84

Pimentel, D., L. Westra, and R.F. Noss. 2000. *Ecological integrity: Integrating environment, conservation, and health.* Washington, DC: Island Press.

Pine, B.J., and James H. Gilmore. 1999. *The experience economy: Work is theatre & every business a stage.* Massachusetts: Harvard Business Press.

Pitney Bowes Inc. 2008. "The Environmental Impact of Mail: A Baseline." Pitney Bowes Inc. www.pb.com/docs/US/pdf/Our-Company/Corporate-Responsibility/The-Environmental-Impact-of-Mail-A-Baseline-White-Paper.pdf (2.1.2016).

Pope, J., D. Annandale, and A. Morrison-Saunders. 2004. "Conceptualising sustainability assessment." *Environmental Impact Assessment Review* 24(6):595–616.

Porter, M.E. 1985. *Competitive strategy: Creating and sustaining superior performance.* New York: The Free Press.

Porter, M.E., and M.R. Kramer. 2006. "The link between competitive advantage and corporate social responsibility." *Harvard Business Review* 84(12):78–92.

Porter, M.E., and M.R. Kramer. 2011. "Creating shared value." *Harvard Business Review* 89(1/2):62–77.

Prahalad, C.K., and V. Ramaswamy. 2004. "Co-creation experiences: The next practice in value creation." *Journal of Interactive Marketing* 18(3):5–14.

Prakash, A. 2000. "Responsible care: An assessment." *Business & Society* 39(2):183–209.

Rifkin, J. 2008. "The third industrial revolution." *Engineering & Technology* 3(7):26–27.

Rifkin, J. 2014. *The zero marginal cost society: The internet of things, the collaborative commons, and the eclipse of capitalism.* New York: Palgrave Macmillan.

Ross, D. 2009. "GHG emissions resulting from aircraft travel." V9.2 5/6/2009, Carbon Planet Ltd. www.carbonplanet.com/downloads/ Flight_Calculator_Information_v9.2.pdf (2.1.2016).

Santangelo, G.D. 2001. "The impact of the information and communications technology revolution on the inter-nationalization of corporate technology." *International Business Review* 10(6):701–26.

Shapin, S. 1996. *The scientific revolution.* Chicago: University of Chicago Press.

Shepon, A., T. Israeli, G. Eshel, and R. Milo. 2013. "EcoTime—An intuitive quantitative sustainability indicator utilizing a time metric." Ecological Indicators, 24, 240–5.

Singh, R.K., H.R. Murty, S.K. Gupta, and A.K. Dikshit. 2009. "An overview of sustainability assessment methodologies." *Ecological Indicators* 9(2):189–212.

Spohrer, J., P.P. Maglio, J. Bailey, and D. Gruhl. 2007. "Steps toward a science of service systems." *Computer* 40 (1):71–7.

Spohrer, J., S.L. Vargo, N. Caswell, and P.P. Maglio. 2008. "The service system is the basic abstraction of service science." In *Hawaii International Conference on System Sciences, Proceedings of the 41st Annual.* IEEE.

Spohrer, J. 2011. Whole service. http://service-science.info/archives/1056 (2.1.16).

Spohrer, J., C., Bassano, P. Piciocchi, and M.A.K. Siddike. 2016. "What makes a system smart? wise?" *Proceeding of The 7th International Conference on Applied Human Factors and Ergonomics.* Florida, USA.

Su, K., J. Li, and H. Fu. 2011. "Smart city and the applications." In 2011 *International Conference on Electronics, Communications and Control (ICECC).* pp. 1028–31.

Townsend, A.M. 2013. *Smart cities: Big data, civic hackers, and the quest for a new Utopia.* WW Norton & Company.

Tukker, A. 2004. "Eight types of product-service system: Eight ways to sustainability? Experiences from SusProNet." *Business Strategy Environment* 13(4):246–60.

Vanclay, J.K., J. Shortiss, S. Aulsebrook, A.M. Gillespie, B.C. Howell, R. Johanni, and J. Yates. 2011. "Customer response to carbon labelling of groceries." *Journal of Consumer Policy* 34(1):153–60.

van den Bergh, J. and M. Antal. 2014. "Evaluating alternatives to GDP as measures of social welfare/progress." Working Paper no 56, WWW for Europe.

Vargo S.L., and R.F. Lusch. 2004. "Evolving to a new dominant logic for marketing." *Journal of Marketing* 68:1–17.

Vargo S.L., and R.F. Lusch. 2008. "Service-dominant logic: Continuing the evolution." *Journal of the Academy of Marketing* Science 36(1):1–10.

Vargo, S.L., P.P. Maglio, and M.A. Akaka. 2008. "On value and value co-creation: A service systems and service logic perspective." *European Management Journal* 26(3):145–52.

Vermesan, O., and P. Friess. 2011. *Internet of things-global technological and societal trends from smart environments and spaces to green ICT.* Delft: River Publishers.

Vishnumurthy, V., S. Chandrakumar, and E.G. Sirer. 2003. "Karma: A secure economic framework for peer-to-peer resource sharing." In *Workshop on Economics of Peer-to-Peer Systems* (Vol. 35). California USA.

Vivier, J. 2006. "Mobility in cities database: Better mobility for people worldwide." International Association of Public Transport, Belgium.

Wackernagel, M., and W. Rees. 1998. *Our ecological footprint: reducing human impact on the earth,* No. 9. Gabriola Island: New Society Publishers.

Weber, C.L., J.G. Koomey, H.S. Matthews. 2009. "The energy and climate change impacts of different music delivery methods." *Final report to Microsoft Corporation and Intel Corporation.* http://download.intel.com/pressroom/pdf/cdsvsdownloadsrelease.pdf (2.1.2016).

Weber, R.H., and R. Weber. 2010. *Internet of Things.* New York: Springer.

Wiersum, K.F. 1995. "200 years of sustainability in forestry: Lessons from history." *Environmental Management* 19(3):321–29.

Wilkins, D.A. 1999. "Assessing ecosystem health." *Trends in Ecology & Evolution* 14(2):69.

Wolfson, A., D. Tavor, S. Mark, M. Schermann, and H. Krcmar. 2010. "S³-Sustainability and services science: Novel perspective and challenge." *Service Science* 2(4):216–24.

Wolfson, A., D. Tavor, and S. Mark. 2011. "Sustainable services: The natural mimicry approach." *Journal of Service Science and Management* 4(2):125–31.

Wolfson, A., D. Tavor, and S. Mark. 2012. "Sustainability and shifting from a 'Person to Person' to a Super- or Self-service." *International Journal of u- and e- Service, Science and Technology* 5(1):25–34.

Wolfson, A., D. Tavor, and S. Mark. 2013a. "Editorial Column—From CleanTech to CleanServ." *Service Science* 5(3):193–96.

Wolfson, A., D. Tavor, and S. Mark. 2013b. "Sustainability as service." *Sustainability Accounting, Management and Policy Journal* 4(1):103–114.

Wolfson, A., D. Tavor, and S. Mark. 2014. "CleanServs: clean services for a more sustainable world." *Sustainability Accounting, Management and Policy Journal* 5(4):405–24.

Wolfson, A., S. Mark, P.M. Martin, and D. Tavor. 2015. *Sustainability through Service: Perspectives, Concepts and Examples.* Heidelberg: Springer.

World Business Council for Sustainable Development. 2000. *Eco-efficiency: Creating more with less.* Retrieved from www.wbcsd.org/web/publications/eco_efficiency_creating_more_value.pdf

World Wildlife Foundation. Carbon footprint calculator, http://footprint.wwf.org.uk/questionnaires/show/1/1/1 (2.1.16).

Xia, F., L.T. Yang, L. Wang, and A. Vinel. 2012. "Internet of Things." *International Journal of Communication Systems* 25(9):1101–2.

Index

OTHER TITLES IN OUR SERVICE SYSTEMS AND INNOVATIONS IN BUSINESS AND SOCIETY COLLECTION

Jim Spohrer, IBM and Haluk Demirkan, Arizona State University, *Editors*

- *Matching Services to Markets: The Role of the Human Sensorium in Shaping Service-Intensive Markets* by H.B. Casanova
- *People, Processes, Services, and Things: Using Services Innovation to Enable the Internet of Everything* by Hazim Dahir, Bil Dry, and Carlos Pignataro
- *Service Design and Delivery: How Design Thinking Can Innovate Business and Add Value to Society* by Toshiaki Kurokawa
- *All Services, All the Time: How Business Services Serve Your Business* by Doug McDavid
- *Modeling Service Systems* by Ralph D. Badinelli
- *Obtaining Value from Big Data for Service Delivery* by Stephen H. Kaisler, Frank Armour, J. Alberto Espinosa and William H. Money
- *Service Innovation* by Anders Gustafsson, Per Kristensson, Gary Schirr, and Lars Witell

Announcing the Business Expert Press Digital Library

Concise e-books business students need for classroom and research

This book can also be purchased in an e-book collection by your library as

- a one-time purchase,
- that is owned forever,
- allows for simultaneous readers,
- has no restrictions on printing, and
- can be downloaded as PDFs from within the library community.

Our digital library collections are a great solution to beat the rising cost of textbooks. E-books can be loaded into their course management systems or onto student's e-book readers.

The **Business Expert Press** digital libraries are very affordable, with no obligation to buy in future years. For more information, please visit **www.businessexpertpress.com/librarians**. To set up a trial in the United States, please contact **sales@businessexpertpress.com**.

www.ingramcontent.com/pod-product-compliance
Lightning Source LLC
Chambersburg PA
CBHW071858200326
41519CB00016B/4449